FOLLOWERS IN THE WAY

FOLLOWERS IN THE WAY

By

H. F. B. MACKAY

NEW YORK
THE MACMILLAN COMPANY
1934

62298

PREFACE

THIS is a collection of addresses mostly given at All Saints', Margaret Street, in the last few years. They may be useful for reading at Retreat meals. I venture to dedicate the collection to my friend, Sidney Dark, as an expression of gratitude for very many kindnesses.

H. F. B. M.

ALL SAINTS',
  MARGARET STREET.
The Octave of St. John the Evangelist, 1934.

CONTENTS

FOLLOWERS IN THE WAY

GAIUS

The elder unto the well-beloved Gaius whom I love in the truth.

3 St. John 1.

IN the first four chapters of this book I want to try to take you into a part of the New Testament which I think has been less explored than the rest, the part associated with St. John. Of the figures I have chosen, Gaius, Diotrephes, and Antipas the Martyr all belong to the story of St. John. One only, Demas, who represents a type of person common to all ages of the Church, was of the circle of St. Paul.

The literature of those last days of the Apostolic times consists of the Book of the Revelation, the three Epistles of St. John and the Gospel of St. John. The Book of the Revelation sets out in the Jewish mystical language, which all Christians in Asia Minor could read (we should call it a kind of cypher), the frightful experience in store for the Church in the following centuries. The Epistles to the seven typical Churches in Asia Minor, which are inserted in the beginning of the Book, are really a preface intended to introduce to the faithful the Book of the Revelation. The three Epistles and the Gospel contain the last message of the Holy Spirit through the sacred scriptures. These last scenes of the Bible are laid in Asia Minor; the centre of action because of its practical convenience is Ephesus; the source of the inspiration is St. John. To concern oneself with the question as to how much of all this the Apostle wrote himself is like asking how many of Titian's pictures show traces of the hands of his pupils, how much of the plays are the work of Shakespeare; interesting secondary questions, but unaffecting that glory which is Titian, that miracle of vision and insight which is Shakespeare. No one but the Apostle John himself was capable of endowing the Church with the so-called books of St. John.

How did the Christians spread the Church during this period? Through the labours of two sets of people. First the messengers who travelled backwards and forwards through the known world, not only the Apostles, Apostolic delegates and prophets, the first rank of the Ministry who exercised Christ's authority throughout the Church, but an immense band of subordinates who carried the writings through which Christian knowledge was conveyed from place to place. Secondly, the hosts, the substantial people in the various cities who offered the brethren hospitality, and bade them warm their hands wherever they went at the hearth-fires of Christian loving comradeship. Some of these were chief ministers of the Christian assemblies—the local presbyters. Others were substantial laymen who had the goodwill and also the power to use hospitality towards the messengers without grudging.

In all this plan of action the Church was very naturally modelling herself on the lines of the Empire itself, and later on this had far-reaching results. After the Roman Empire broke into pieces the art of writing fell largely into abeyance, but in the great highly civilized world of the first century it was the chief instrument of government. The Empire was maintained by means of rescripts, letters and memoranda. The transmission of letters was very easy. The ease, certainty and comfort of travel were wonderful. It was slow, of course, but never so comfortable again until the days of our great liners. So the world was being constantly traversed by messengers of government carrying Imperial rescripts and the communications between the authorities which kept the world knit together, and by the letter carriers, *tabellarii*, as they were called, of the great trading companies who conveyed orders between the firms in Rome and their branches throughout the world.

But strangely enough, and most fortunately for the Church, there was no general post. Fortunately, because it compelled the Church to create a postal system of her own. It was her postal system which knit the Church on earth into one communion and fellowship. In the Apostolic letters, authoritative like the Imperial rescripts, were contained the saving truths of the Church, and in their circulation flowed her life blood. The messengers could not be sent to pagan inns, and an immense system of hospitality had to be organized for them. This duty fell upon the heads and principal personages of the Christian communities and brought them into touch with the communities from which the messengers came, and to which they went. In this way the ministers of local churches, instead of keeping themselves to themselves, and knowing nothing of their neighbours, became guardians of the unity of the Church Catholic and of the channels through which her life blood flowed.

I said this came to have far-reaching results. Gradually the Empire became conscious of the existence of the ever-growing framework of a society which refused to recognize the divine character of the Imperial power, a silently hostile *imperium in imperio*. The Empire came to hate it as the development of a real antagonist, a rival

GAIUS

administration. So too, in later days when the
Empire began to fall to pieces, Constantine saw
that here stood revealed, strong and compact,
another organization, the Church, ready to take its
place.

Now at the end of the first century in glorious
Ephesus, under the shadow of the Temple of
Artemis, whose golden roofs, they tell us, shone
from afar like a star across the sea, there continued
to live a very old man, surrounded by a band of
adoring disciples, the old, old Apostle John. He
was very old, but from the moment when he first
asked his Lord " Master, where dwellest Thou ? "
he had been reserved to do for the Church at the
end of the century the work he was now doing.
Peter and Paul were in their graves. Their work
at Rome was being unobtrusively carried on by
Linus, Cletus, and Clement. Clement had written
a letter in the name of the Roman Church to the
heads of the Church in Corinth, begging them to
compose their differences. But neither Peter nor
Paul, much less Linus, Cletus or Clement, was
designed to bring the Church to accept the fact
made clear by the persecution under Domitian that
the Church would be forced in the second century to refuse divine honours, not merely to all
that was worst in the world but to all that was
best.

It needed the Son of Thunder to do that and he was now doing it. From his Apostolic Throne in Ephesus his messengers went throughout the churches of Asia Minor, and here we have a letter from the Apostle to one of their hosts, an important official of a daughter church in what we may, by a convenient anachronism, call the ecclesiastical province of Asia.

We poor moderns would consider the place into which they had come extraordinarily beautiful, but it was an unfriendly place for them. No longer did the messengers appeal to the Jews. That day is over, and St. John, who never minces matters, now calls them the synagogue of Satan. Nor could they hold much converse with the pagans, but in every city there was now a Christian assembly making its supernatural power felt. It would meet in some big house, and on the loving kindness and hospitality of that big house the Church's mission to the world largely depended.

I see Gaius like an Apostolic Thomas More reading his letter surrounded by his wife and children and household. " The Elder," says the Apostle, " to the well-beloved Gaius whom I love in the Truth." Mark, the Faith has now become the Truth. The Truth, the central, permanent core of doctrine and practice flowing from the fact of the Incarnation now revealed to their fullest

14

extent in the writings of the Apostle John. The
life of Gaius is the fruit of this.

"Beloved," says the old man, "I wish above all
things that you may prosper and be in health, even
as your soul prospers. May your public and social
work for the Church prosper as your own spiritual
life prospers." It has been thought that one
reason which moved St. John to write the letter
was that some illness or accident had lately crippled
Gaius' work.

"I am delighted when from time to time brethren
come and bear witness of your truth." As we
shall see later on, there was trouble in the local
church. The trouble had required occasional
reports to the Apostle, and the messengers had
always reported the perfect and sincere loyalty with
which Gaius maintained the fullness of Catholic
Faith and Practice. "Yes, indeed, you live as you
teach. God gives me no greater grace than the
free gift of the joy of such tidings that I may hear
of mine own children walking in the Truth."

Then in a little illustration from the conduct of
Gaius, St. John shows the practical character of the
Christian life, which is not lived dreaming after
the God revealed in Nature or in grace, but which
can only be lived in the give and take of the
Christian society. Some members of the travelling
ministry had come to the place and there had been

FOLLOWERS IN THE WAY

some unworthy opposition to their reception, but Gaius had gladly taken them into his house. So St. John goes on : " Dear friend, there can never fail of God's blessing whatsoever you do for the brethren, and there is an added beauty in this if the brethren are strangers. They bore witness to your loving kindness before the Assembly at Ephesus." (These missionaries had evidently expressed their gratitude to Gaius on some public occasion at which the Apostle had been present.)

He goes on to say, " They will be coming again, and it will be a blessing if you will forward them on their journey in a manner worthy of their dedication to the service of God ; for they went out for the Name's sake " (think what that phrase meant to the writer), " refusing to accept alms from the unconverted Gentiles." A great sentence—giving us a vision of a great adventure. " We are bound," he adds, "to support such, that we may be fellow-workers with the Truth."

The joy of the Elder and the strength of the Elder—how beautiful it is ! We saw it in Bishop King, in Father Congreve, in Father Wainwright, in Father Brett, in Canon Carter. Men saw it wonderfully in John Keble, whose face became radiant in old age, like an illuminated clock, as the grace shone through.

The joy of St. John was at the spectacle of Gaius,

a man who had made his heart a chapel of the Truth, and his home a church of the Truth, and had welcomed all who loved the Good Tidings into his heart and home.

DEMAS

Demas hath forsaken me, having loved this present world, and is departed from me to Thessalonica.

2 Timothy iv, 9.

ST. PAUL wrote these words a short time before his death. He had been arrested, probably at Troas in Asia Minor, as one of the chiefs of the Christian Church in Rome, conveyed to Rome probably via Corinth and Brindisi, and he is now confined in a dungeon, tradition says of the Mamertine prison. During the earlier imprisonment from which he had been released, he had lived in his own flat, and had been surrounded by friends. This time he knew the end had come, and it seemed a very dreary end. He was going to be executed, not for the Faith, but on the ridiculous charge that his followers had tried to burn down the city. He had not been in Rome for some time, and the Roman Christians, who were keeping hidden as much as they could, and apparently somewhere had St. Peter in concealment, were afraid to go and see him. Of his big following of disciples only Luke was with him.

Dr. Lock, than whom nobody had a more subtle

appreciation of St. Paul's Greek, paraphrases the passage as follows : " Make every effort to come speedily ; I am very lonely, Demas has deserted me ; his heart was set not on the appearing of the Lord, but on what this world can offer, and he went off to Thessalonica ; Cresceus is gone to Galatia, Titus to Dalmatia. Luke is with me, but he is single-handed. Pick up Mark on your journey and bring him with yourself; for he is most useful, always ready for any service. As for Tychicus, I am sending him to Ephesus. The cloak which I left behind at Troas with Carpus bring with you when you come, also my papers, but above all I want the rolls " (possibly the rolls were Gospels).

St. Paul is in a dungeon and about to die, but he is as busy and practical as ever. He is also as sensitive, as human as ever, the childlike element is as strong in him as ever, and certainly he was no stoic.

This passage is a good illustration of the fact I pointed out in the last chapter, that those who were behaving as our Lord's active disciples in the world were organized at that time into a great system of hosts and messengers.

In Gaius we looked at a host who succeeded, in Demas we look at a messenger who failed.

Demas or Demetrius—it is another form of that name—was a Greek Christian. Bishop Lightfoot does not doubt that he was a Thessalonian by birth, and that what happened was that he gave up his share in the mission to the world and went home. St. Paul had never been able to do much at Thessalonica after his first visit, because of the riot which ensued. The authorities had undertaken not to be harsh if the Christians would undertake to keep Paul away from the place. On the other hand the enthusiasm of the Thessalonian converts had been great, they were living in so enthusiastic an expectation of an immediate and glorious Second Coming of Christ that they were concerned lest those who had died should not share in the great event, and St. Paul had to reassure them and correct them. " Be ambitious to be quiet and attend to the ordinary affairs of daily life." That is part of his advice to them in the letters to the Thessalonians.

I fancy that this was the situation out of which Demas came, joined Paul and became one of his assistant messengers. He must have been with him off and on for a considerable time, and he was evidently with St. Paul through his time at Ephesus. He was one of those who helped him during his first Roman imprisonment. In the Epistles Paul wrote at that time he singles out the names of his companions whom the Christians he was writing to knew, and includes them in his salutations. St. Paul had not been to Colosse at the time when he

wrote the epistle to the Colossians, so he had never
visited the wealthy Philemon to whom he wrote
interceding for the dishonest runaway slave,
Onesimus, but in both the letters to Colosse and
to Philemon he includes the name of Demas.
Evidently Demas had been one of the messengers
whom St. Paul sent from his side at Ephesus to work
at Colosse—" Greeting also," he writes to the
Colossians, " from Luke the Physician, my dearly
loved friend, and from Demas." The conduct of
those two men is put in direct contrast in my text,
" Demas forsook me, only Luke is with me." Is
that foreshadowed in the salutation years before in
which Luke is spoken of with special tenderness
and Demas dismissed with a mere mention ?

In the Apocryphal Acts of Paul and Thecla,
Demas appears as a jealous and treacherous companion of St. Paul; the historian, Epiphanius, in
his work on the Heresies, calls him an apostate.
But I should question his having been either. I
do not think we know more about him than the
New Testament tells us. Demas is a man who fell
under the temptation which almost every man,
woman and child who reads these words has felt,
the temptation to " give up "—Demas gave up.
He simply, I imagine, could not stand it any longer.
He had been at least off and on with St. Paul for
years. After the first imprisonment he had joined

him again. It must have been on their way through Greece towards Rome that he left him and turned north to Thessalonica.

St. Paul did not in the least wish to induce his friends to put themselves into Nero's hands ; our Lord's directions had been to avoid martyrdom as long as possible. Erastus, who had been treasurer of Corinth, an important person, was left there as they went through to Brindisi ; Tychicus was sent back with despatches to Ephesus; Cresceus and Titus were given missions to Galatia and Dalmatia. But with Demas it was another matter ; he gave up his work as messenger and retired into private life. It was a desertion, he forsook St. Paul and all the work connected with St. Paul. We can best convey the situation in slang, if we say that he was completely fed up, he gave it all up, he felt he could not stick it any longer.

I do not think his nerve gave way. I think he felt that the whole thing had been a ghastly disappointment, that the expectations had all been exaggerated. How absurd, he felt, had been those anxieties about the dead his fellow Thessalonians had felt which St. Paul had soothed in a letter !— Second Coming indeed, there had been no Second Coming—everybody was turning against the Christian religion everywhere ; the situation got not better but worse. He was one of the first of the

people described in the Second Epistle of Peter
who were beginning in their hearts at least to
ridicule the Christian hope, and saying, " Where
is the promise of His coming ? for since the Fathers
fell asleep all things continue as they were from the
beginning of creation."

The first great opposition, the opposition of the
Jews, would not concern Demas very much, and
he must always have been prepared for the opposition of great local cults like the cult of Artemis at
Ephesus, but when the Empire itself began to turn
against the Church it was a very different matter.
It had not quite happened yet. It is not until
we get into the next two chapters that we have
to face what began in the reign of Domitian, but
the absurd false charge at Rome showed the way
the wind was blowing, and why in the world
should a decent Thessalonian be mixed up in a false
charge levelled against the Christians of Rome ?
No, Demas went back to Thessalonica.

He is really one of the commonest of all pheno-
mena, an average man who cannot go the whole
way. Of course there are dramatic, tragic illus-
trations of men who have, as they say, and we say,
" given everything up," people who have acted
treacherously, people who have apostatized as the
Acts of Paul and Thecla and Epiphanius say Demas
did. But I do not take him that way ; I take him

23

as a warning that I and perhaps some of you need much more, I take him as the man who could not go the whole way with Christ, who had once been a messenger but had thought it too much for him and had settled back at home with the intention no doubt of living a respectable life amid surroundings mostly pagan.

There are many hosts and messengers of Christ among our readers; thank God for that. Brethren, each one of you was once a messenger of Christ. You came to be solemnly enrolled, you stood before the Apostle—the Bishop—and he said to you, " Do you here in the presence of God and of this congregation renew the solemn promise and vow that was made in your name at your baptism, ratifying and confirming the same in your own persons, and acknowledging yourselves bound to believe and to do all those things which your godfathers and godmothers then undertook for you ? "

And audibly you answered " I do." Then you knelt before the Apostle and you felt upon your head the strong pressure of Apostolic Authority which equipped you and sealed you for the great adventure. And soon after you gave to your pastors one of the most moving of all their experiences, you lifted towards them the innocent and reverent faces of dear children, and they laid on your young lips the Body and Blood of the Lord.

24

And since then? Well, there has been the Christian warfare which you went away that spring morning to encounter, equipped as Knights of the Holy Grail. And there has inevitably been the temptation to be fed up with it, not to stick it, to give it all up. But it has always been possible to go on with St. Paul, and it is possible for some time at least to go back to St. Paul. Think of the joy to St. Paul if he could have got a letter from Demas next morning, saying, "I am so sorry, so very sorry, I am coming back."

Sometimes I happen to look at the prayer-desk in the confessional, and I see lying on it an utterly tattered and worn-out dirty brown and threadbare book. It is the manual given to the penitent at his confirmation, almost entirely destroyed by its long use in prayer. What a lovely sight! It is like the marble slab in the Holy Sepulchre on the place where the Lord lay, which I once kissed, and which has been worn into waves by the kisses of the pilgrims. You know how some of you have sometimes said, "I can bear it no longer, I am going to give everything up." But you never really meant it. No, no, you are going to journey on with St. Paul.

You know that nothing matters for you in your Christian life but Prayer, Patience and Perseverance. They will bring you to a good death and nothing else matters. A good death. I remember one in the Middlesex Hospital, the death of one of our All Saints' children. I watched the doctors and students as they stood round her bed, and their reverence and tenderness remain one of my most beautiful memories. When I went up to her I found her face lit up with a radiant smile. " You are very happy, Annie," I said. She nodded, for she was nearly gone. Then she made a big effort and said, still smiling radiantly, " Oh, I am so glad I am in the Confraternity." For Annie had remained with St. Paul.

DIOTREPHES

I wrote unto the Church; but Diotrephes, who loveth
to have the pre-eminence among them, receiveth us not—
Wherefore if I come, I will remember his deeds which he
doeth, prating against us with malicious words : and not
content therewith, neither doth he himself receive the
brethren, and forbiddeth them that would, and casteth them
out of the Church.   Beloved, follow not that which is evil
but that which is good.   He that doeth good is of God :
but he that doeth evil hath not seen God.   Demetrius hath
good report of all men and of the truth itself : yea and
we also bear record; and ye know that our record is true.
—I had many things to write, but I will not with ink and
pen write unto thee : But I trust I shall shortly see thee
and we shall speak face to face.   Peace be to thee—our
friends salute thee.   Greet the friends by name.

3 St. John 9–14.

WE are back again at the end of the First
Century in the reign of Domitian.   The
Church is beginning to encounter the dangers of
crossing the bar between the Apostolic and the
sub-Apostolic age.   It is an age of intense Christian vitality, when the Church is becoming a vast
network of intercommunications.   A system of
hosts and messengers is making the Church already
something of an *imperium in imperio.*   The Empire
is beginning to hate her for her growing power.

Already some dim, slight outline is appearing of that system which will replace the Empire as the cohesive force of civilization when the Empire begins to break into pieces.

In the last days of St. John, therefore, all faithful Christians were missionaries, either messengers or the hosts of messengers. The self-contained, easy-going life of modern Christians was a thing unimaginable. We have studied a host who succeeded—Gaius—and a messenger who failed—Demas; now let us look at a host who failed to give that Christ-like hospitality of mind and heart, of hearth and home, which is an absolutely essential element in the Church's life.

The controversies referred to in the New Testament were chiefly not between Christian and Pagan, or Christian and Jew, but between Apostolic Christianity and various other forms of Christianity; generally the controversy was over doctrine, sometimes it was over morals, sometimes over the question of authority.

The story of Diotrephes is the story of disobedience and false ambition within the Church's circle. What sort of man was this gentleman whom St. John castigates in his third epistle, using language as strong as our Lord's denunciation of some of the Pharisees? He appears to have been the local presbyter, the " parish priest " of this

28

community, as Gaius was one of its leading laymen. He was evidently a man of ability, position and means, not a slacker, an ardent member of the Church, upholding her moral standards among heathen surroundings; a man, therefore, who prayed, fasted, and gave alms, who was keenly interested in the progress of Christianity, who aspired to be the guiding spirit of this local church, and had succeeded in reaching the most influential position in it—not, remember, in a worldly, comfortable, luxurious Church, not in a body which might well attract a worldly man. This was no Renaissance cardinal, no Cardinal Bibbiena or Cardinal Bembo; this happened in the little Christian community of the Apostolic age, despised and rejected of men, the people who for the sake of the Incarnation were losing their all and facing a hostile world.

It was this community that Diotrephes was ambitious to lead, and was leading in a spirit alien from Christ. An eager member of this strenuous band, he had yet rejected St. John's letter and direction and had attacked the exercise of Apostolic authority. He had not attacked the name of Christ; he had attacked the Apostolic ministry in the name of Christ, and not content with words, had put himself out of communion with the people who had been loyal and had entertained the messengers who had come with the commendation of St. John. St. John speaks in the plainest terms — Diotrephes had prated against the Catholic authorities with malicious words. St. John is coming himself before long and he is going to deal drastically with Diotrephes. It is a sad story.

To have been a Christian at all he must have been to a large extent faithful, prayerful, self-sacrificing, mortified, and yet with this anti-Christian result. His prayer had been turned into sin. What a tragedy !

There is not, there never has been, an ideal Christian society ; mankind must have become sinless before that is possible. Our Lord had warned his disciples on Maundy Thursday night that nothing in the future would be so difficult as the relationships of the inner circle. Here was a party, a group among these good people, honestly convinced that Diotrephes was right and St. John was wrong. Both men were enthusiastic, but now we know that St. John was right and Diotrephes was wrong and we know why. St. John had the essence of the matter in him, and Diotrephes had not ; there was a third party behind the scenes as there always is — our Lord — and St. John had our Lord on his side and Diotrephes had not. It is not enough to array oneself under our Lord's banner ; one must have given oneself to him body, mind and spirit as well. Otherwise, under the banner of Christ, a force alien to Him will be arrayed, and one which therefore will be His unconscious enemy all the time—such was Diotrephes.

On the other hand St. John had acquired so much of our Lord's character, temper, tone, methods ; he was so entirely absorbed not by the Christian programme merely, but by Christ himself, that when he had to deal with controversy as to what the programme involved and what it did not, he did not go wrong. His union with our Lord gave him the true instincts, the right point of view.

What was the point at issue ? It is not stated in the epistle, but I do not think it was the tremendous question with which we are to deal in the next chapter, as to whether it would be possible to find some *modus vivendi* with the Empire, and escape persecution. I think it was probably a matter of personal jealousy and pettiness over the relation of the messengers to the local clergy, the sort of difficulty which arose again in the Middle Ages between the parochial clergy and the friars. Its pettiness made it the more disgraceful ; it was poisoning the Church's life, spoiling the beauty and peace of the community, depressing, disheartening the messengers.

Diotrephes is the Church's greatest hindrance in every age, the tiresome, self-assertive, un-

Christian Christian. I have sometimes thought that it might be a good thing if the clergy would publish in their parish magazines a selection of the letters they have received from Diotrephes in order to expose this corrupt vein in Christian community life in a strong light. What is at the root of it? Freud would tell us sex, and although Freud lays far too great a stress on sex, I believe that in this case Freud is right. The ardent Christian is called upon by his religion to discipline his sex instincts very strictly. They must in many cases either be suppressed or sublimated. If they are sublimated they bear fruit in pastoral tenderness, if they are suppressed they show themselves in envy, hatred, malice and all uncharitableness. Frustrated sex engaged in theological controversy is not a pretty spectacle.

But it will be more useful if we give to the story of Diotrephes a closer personal application. In so far as we are not altogether the followers of our Lord we have all got a strain of Diotrephes in us. The Christian is sometimes puzzled as to how far he may use his personality. He must take the line and defend the position he firmly believes in, and he knows that his personality is the instrument given to him for the purpose. The wall of the City of God has twelve foundations, and in them are the names, that is to say, the personalities, of the twelve Apostles of the Lamb, each unique, but all, mark it, a harmony, and taken together a design. None of the twelve must be out of proportion, of the wrong colour, out of place. How shall we know whether we are harmoniously in place ? St. John helps us. Here is St. John using authority, asserting himself, using strong words, but observe Diotrephes has thrust himself up, while St. John has a duty to act, a duty to keep order. Diotrephes enjoys arguing. St. John does not. There is no love behind the action of Diotrephes, there is love behind the action of St. John. There is the test— is my incisiveness, my sternness, inspired by love or is it not ? Scott Holland has recalled to us the stern glint which sometimes flashed from Bishop King's blue eyes, beneath his level brows, and I well remember how formidable the strictness of his questioning seemed while as a Governor of Pusey House he catechized me, a young Librarian, about the desirability of a large and beautiful chapel for the work of Pusey House. He would have given short shrift to Diotrephes.

Think what a difference it would make if you and I had never to reveal any " Diotrephes," when we make our confessions. Think what a lot of room Diotrephes takes up in many people's con-fessions. We cannot get rid of Diotrephes in our own strength ; we can only get rid of him altogether by plunging ourselves into the love of God, opening our hearts to the love of God, giving ourselves to preach and live the love of God in the home, in the office, in the shop, in the work-room.

That is not done by aiming at a Christ-like pose, but by doing Christ-like things, making the imitation of Christ in little things the effort of every day.

Gradually the spirit of Diotrephes gets put over the doorstep of our hearts, and St. John is left in possession.

ANTIPAS

Antipas my faithful martyr.

Revelation ii. 12–17.

FIFTEEN miles from the Mediterranean Sea, which it overlooks across the broad plain of the Caicus, stands a huge rocky hill, designed by nature to bear a royal city. The city it came to bear was called Pergamos. Its people were skilled in the preparation of skins for writing materials and from Pergamena comes our word parchment.

Like all the rest of Asia Minor, Pergamos had been fought over by various dynasties, until in the year 133 before Christ the Roman Empire brought it peace by converting the whole region into the Roman Province of Asia. Owing to the majesty of its natural position the Romans made Pergamos the official capital of the province. Here the first, and for a long time the only, altar and temple in the whole province of Asia, were raised to the veneration of the Empire and the Emperor ; hither flocked the people of the province to offer their gratitude, homage and love to Augustus and his successors, the saviours of their world, to them the source and embodiment of the highest good they knew.

But at the end of the First Christian Century there was still living in Ephesus an old man who had been detained on earth to fight this good, a good which was then proving itself to be the enemy of the better. Mark how St. John does it. He is leading the Church to submit to persecution from the Augustan power which was the world's peace, and he does this by rousing the Church into opposition against it. He proscribes and condemns the Augustan power and peace, the best thing which so far the world had ever known. St. John will have no grey tints in his landscape, only black and white ; he declares that now that the better has come, the hitherto good in opposing it has become the bad —" All these things will I give thee," Satan had said to Jesus on the high mountain, " all the Augustan power and peace, if with an obeisance of courtesy thou wilt take them from my hand," and the Christ had answered, " Get thee behind me, Satan, thou shalt worship the Lord thy God and Him only shalt thou serve."

And so to the angel of the Church of Pergamos, the Church in the official capital of the Roman authority in the province of Asia, our Lord now speaks through the Apostle John. He speaks as the authority which is come to destroy the Roman authority—" These things saith he that hath the sharp-pointed two-edged sword (that means the

36

power of life and death), I know where thou dwellest, where Satan's throne is." For in all ages Satan
is the power which withstands the Church and all
that belongs to it, and so in the Augustan Temple
at Pergamos Satan sits enthroned.

Nowhere then was the issue made so clear as at
Pergamos ; and up the great hill from all parts of
the province a thin stream in chains was moving to
bear faithful witness that there is another name
greater than Augustus, the name of Jesus. Great
was the devotion of the Church in Pergamos to the
name of Jesus, but within her ranks there was a
Nicolaitan group joining issue with the old Apostle
as to the lawfulness of taking part in the Imperial
ritual. As this group of superior and broad-minded
persons watched the line of Christian martyrs
being brought up the hill in chains to suffer for
the Name's sake, they were tempted to say, " To
what purpose is this waste ? We are all good
citizens of the Empire ; why decline the current
test of good citizenship, why not burn a little
incense to the Emperor ? A little incense is nothing
at all."

But St. John answers, " Cæsar is claiming to be
the Highest Good ; as such Cæsar is the enemy
of Jesus. Whosoever exalts the Holy Name is
not Cæsar's friend ; whosoever makes Jesus his
King speaketh against Cæsar."

Nothing short of this inexorable line would have brought about the persecutions, and the martyrs were necessary to the progress of redemption. The Church must take up the Cross and follow Christ to Calvary that she might fill up that which was lacking of the sufferings of Christ. Christ cannot redeem mankind without a following ; mankind is redeemed through the continual witness of His followers.

In every Christian age and in every Christian life this element of martyrdom appears. Twice in my lifetime it has appeared in the form it took in the Apostolic age. It has involved the destruction of the Armenian people ; we have seen a nation die for the faith. It has involved the slaughter of thousands of faithful Christians in Russia, where the force St. John calls Satan is trying to create the most scientific pagan world mankind has yet imagined. (The world Russia is trying to create is described in Mr. Aldous Huxley's recent book, *Brave New World*, which I notice the Irish Free State has banned. I do not wish it banned in England, for while I do not see why Christian ladies should be offended by reading this book, I think men of discretion should read it with careful attention.)

But most of us have not the painful exhilaration of facing the pagan power as an external enemy.

It penetrated the Church when the Empire flooded it in the Fourth Century, and ever since it has been the Christian's lot to seek to thrust it out of his own being and out of his own Christian environment. We must not complain of this, it is the Divine plan; the Church is designed to be the leaven which is to work in the world until the whole is leavened, and it was for the purity of this leaven that St. John was fighting. Had it made a bargain with the Empire it would have lost its quality. But when the world had been brought to its knees by the witness of the Church under persecution, and the Emperor and his court begged for admission, the Church had to take mankind in, to take it in the bulk and seek to transform it.

It marred the beauty of the Church. People approached the means of grace with faulty motives. It brought the Church into league with politics, her unearthliness was obscured, and the Empire penetrated into individual character, lowered the Christian's sexual standard, tempted man's worldly ambitions, and installed its favourites in high ecclesiastical places. These are some of the chains which the spirit of Cæsar has hung to-day upon those who would climb the steep ascent of heaven.

It is weary work to climb in chains. St. John reminds us of our three great encouragements. In exchange for the pagan jollities which we are called upon to renounce we have the hidden manna. More and more as life goes on we shall feel the sweetness, power and peace of that most Blessed Sacrament. And we possess what our Bibles call the white stone, the white tessera, by which is meant the little tablet like a white marble domino which the Ancients used as tokens of admission to circles of great privilege, and ours is the Communion of Saints, loving intimacy with the best men and women of the last two thousand years, the best men and women who have ever lived. And thirdly, the watchword of a new name, infinitely more glorious than Augustus, that name of Jesus which is above every name, that name at which every knee shall bow, of things in heaven and things in earth and things under the earth.

So I take Antipas as representing everybody before me now who perseveres to the end. He was not alone in his witness. St. John tells us that already the Imperial authority was drunk with the blood of the faithful, but there was a distinction about this man which induces St. John to make him representative of all. He was probably not a man of Pergamos ; Pergamos was the Tyburn of the province of Asia, where people from all sides were brought to die at the shrine of the Augustan power : travelling to death for long days through that lovely land bathed in the southern sun, happy in the

Augustan plenty and wrapt in the Augustan peace.

And now he reaches the last stage and sets foot on the huge and rocky hill crowned with the royal city. The higher he goes the wider is the landscape which the view unfolds to him, the further below him is the world he is leaving; its beauty seems sweeter, as all our memories do the further they are left behind, the Augustan peace seems more profound.

Antipas—we look at him as he pauses and lifts his chained arm to wipe the sweat from his face, the unknown warrior of the Apocalypse of whom we only know the one essential thing, that like Cæsar's Christian page who wrote on the wall of the page boys' common room in the Palace on the Palatine, "Anaxamenos fidelis," that Antipas was faithful —faithful to the end.

Who is Antipas? If you persevere, you are Antipas. Yes, if you persevere and get at last to the top. You are bound with the chain of your sins, you say, those venial sins which hinder your path. Never mind, you can climb notwithstanding, they will be struck off you at the top. Go on, you are receiving the secret strength, you are armed with the white token, you are on the hillside. On to the summit and complete your faithful witness to the Name of Names.

Antipas—Where is he to-night?
Hidden from the darkness of our mortal sight,
Hidden in the Paradise of lovely light.
Hidden in God's Presence, worshipped face to face,
Hidden in the sanctuary of Christ's embrace.
Up, O Wills! to track him home among the blessed,
Up, O Hearts! to know him in the joy of rest;
Where no darkness more shall hide him from our sight
Where we shall be love with love and light with light,
Worshipping our God together face to face,
Wishless in the sanctuary of Christ's embrace.

THE MARTYRDOMS AT LYONS AND VIENNE

THIS is the story of the sufferings and triumphs of our brethren of the Churches of Lyons and Vienne in France, a hundred years after the time of the Apostles.

The country we now call Asia Minor was the seed bed of Christianity. From there it spread far and wide by land and sea, and as one of the greatest sea routes of those days lay between Ephesus and Marseilles there were soon strong Christian colonies in Marseilles and in the larger towns on the banks of the Rhone. It was in Lyons and Vienne on the banks of the Rhone that these tragic things happened, and when the worst of the persecution was over the Christians sent an epistle to their Mother churches of Asia describing what had befallen them. Eusebius, the historian, embedded this priceless document in his history, and that is how I have contemporary first-hand evidence for what I am going to say.

Before I began to write this paper I looked at a photograph which hangs on my walls, and took down a book from my shelves. The photograph shows the marble bust of a boy, the head, broad-browed, drooping in reverie, the face austere, pensive and beautiful. Of all boys in history, except the Holy Child, I would like best to have known that boy, the young prince of the Palatine, who became the Emperor Marcus Aurelius. The book contained the Emperor's Colloquy with himself which we call *The Meditations of Marcus Aurelius*. Listen to the boy speaking to himself when he began to reign. " Have a care you have not too much of the Emperor in you. Be candid, sincere and modestly grave. Let justice and piety reign in your character, let your temper be known for its mildness and good nature. Strive to be the man that virtue and philosophy desire to make you. Worship the Divine Powers and protect mankind. Life is short : all it can give you is the opportunity of adoring the Powers of Heaven and doing good to those around you. Your father was a religious prince ; imitate him in this, and you will have the peace religion brings in the last hour of your life."

It is strange to reflect that the virtues of that man, one of the noblest men that ever lived, helped to bring their sufferings upon the Christians of Lyons and Vienne. In the previous reign, the reign of the equally noble and virtuous Antoninus Pius, extraordinary calamities through earthquake, fire and flood, had befallen the world, and it became

generally believed that they were the punishments
inflicted on mankind for the atheism of a growing
and obstinate people, a secret sect whose unknown
religion the state would not licence, a people who
refused to worship the gods, and publicly insulted
the Emperor and the state by declining to offer
worship to the Emperor's statues. These people
were called Christians from the name of their
founder and leader, the Arch-Atheist Christus, the
disastrous influence of whose magic was believed
to be interfering with the laws of nature and causing
the calamities which were desolating the world.
These people met in the depths of the night to
perform their rites, which it was understood
involved the crimes of cannibalism, incest and
unnatural vices.   What made men say such things ?
The fact is that men were becoming conscious that
a spiritual power was growing up amongst them
which refused to recognize the gods or the bene-
ficence of the Empire, and which was stronger than
any they knew ; and they decided, since it rejected
the gods, it must be demoniacal.   So you understand why a virtuous Emperor like Marcus Aurelius
takes steps against it, and a vicious Emperor, like
his successor, Commodus, does not trouble to do so.
It was not hatred, it was the stronger power of
deadly fear which armed itself against the Christians
of Lyons and Vienne, a deadly fear which became

an insane popular panic at the sight of the super-human strength and courage of the Christians under torture.

Come, then, to Lyons on some brilliant morning. The city in those days lay on the slope to the right of the two rivers, in the quarter now called Four-vieres, a word derived from *Forum Vetus*, the Old Forum round which the terror raged. Come and watch the thing begin. It begins by the Christian housewife finding that she can buy no eggs to-day, and that the fresh vegetables on the stall at which she deals have been bespoken. She goes home with a bewildered air and an empty basket, to find that her husband has been refused his stoup of wine at the wine shop on the way to work, and that the boys, dashing into the public baths with merry faces, had been told that they could not be admitted.

That was the beginning—a silent boycott. The hostility increased. Christians were forced to keep in their houses, they only appeared in public on urgent necessity. Then the anti-Christian panic broke out into violence. Prominent Christians when sighted were hooted and mobbed, they were pelted and beaten, their clothes were torn off their backs. Next the Tribune and Commandant collected as many as they knew of into the Forum, cross-examined them before a seething mob, and put them into gaol until the Governor could hold an inquiry. The day came when the prisoners stood before the Governor and the City Council accused of sacrilege and high treason.

Then followed a sensation. A well-known citizen, Vettius Epagathus, highly admired and esteemed, stood up in his place and said, " I desire to be heard in defence of the accused."

That a man of repute should take the Christian side so infuriated the Councillors that they shouted him down. When he had got silence, the Governor said to Vettius, " I have only one question to ask you. Are you a Christian ? "

" Yes," said Vettius ; and they fell upon him and killed him there and then.

So the St. Stephen of the story won his crown. The appalling savagery of the act sent a wave of hesitation and fear through the prisoners ; for the first time they realized what they were in for. Ten wavered and failed, the rest stood firm, greatly distressed at the failure of the ten.

There were now three groups of Christians in Lyons, the confessors, the lapsed, and those who had not yet been arrested and were still free men. " The confessors," says the Epistle, " were not afraid of the punishments, but were terribly afraid that the lapse of some would hinder the alacrity of those who had not yet declared themselves." We

47

saw that fear at the beginning of the War, the fear that England would disgrace herself by not coming in. We do not see it to-day in the fight for Christ. Until it reappears in that fight the Church will make no further progress. The undeclared Christians were not in hiding ; they were daily visiting the prisoners in the gaol, and sharing their wretched discomforts, and there was no holding back. The arrests went on, and soon all the best and strongest Christians of Lyons and Vienne were collected in the gaol.

It was against Roman Law to allow a slave to give evidence against his master, but now the heathen slaves of Christian masters were cross-examined under threat of torture, and readily confessed that the Holy Eucharist was an occasion when the worshippers ate human flesh and practised unnatural vices. The origin of this slander is obvious. The Christians had begun to rescue the unwanted babies who were exposed by heathen mothers, and to rear them in the fear and admonition of the Lord ; while perversions of the Catholic doctrine of the Eucharist had got abroad, and it was reported that the babies supplied the menus of the cannibal banquets.

These stories were readily believed. Old friends who had hitherto been silent turned bitterly against the prisoners, and the authorities thought it their duty to apply the torture to these enemies of the human race.

The first confessors who stand out before us in a clear light are Blandina, a slave girl, and Sanctus, a deacon of the Church of Vienne. There is no modern parallel to Blandina, who was a slave doing the most menial work behind the scenes in a big house, too ugly and stunted and wizened to appear before her family. A pale-cheeked child with wretched health. Her mistress, also a confessor, could not believe she could bear a single torturing touch. But Blandina, by her stubbornness, wearied the torturers out, and they threw her back into prison one living, bleeding wound. Sanctus, on the other hand, was a splendid young man. When they had done to him all they had done to Blandina, they applied red-hot plates of brass to his body, and burned away its most sensitive parts. Distorted into a knot, he had ceased to look like a human being when he was brought back to prison. They kept him for three days, his body so much inflamed that it could not be touched, and then took him out and applied the torture to the same places again. " He will die this time," they said, " and strike fear into the rest." But with the second application of torture Sanctus revived. He lifted up his bent head and straightened out his crooked back, his old appearance and the use of his limbs returned. The torturers saw that they were healing Sanctus, and they put him back into his dungeon.

Among the lapsed there was one pathetic woman, an arrant coward, who had amused the heathen by her terror. Her name was Biblias, and the authorities thought it desirable, although it was against the law, to give her a taste of the torture that the people might hear her confess publicly the truth of the crimes charged against the Christians; but with the first touch of the torture Biblias awoke to the glory she had nearly missed. She denied the crimes, she confessed the Christ, she was raised to a Martyr's throne, and we know that all the trumpets sounded for her on the other side.

The alarming constancy of the martyrs now brought the public torturing to a standstill. It was feared that it might have a bad effect on the people, so the next scenes were enacted in the lowest dungeons of the prison. In vaults without light and air the prisoners were put into the stocks which stretched the body to a point of ceaseless agony. Here our Lord intervened. He quickly took to Himself all the boy and girl prisoners and all the newly arrested, for they all sank and died at once. On the other hand He strengthened His veterans. They kept cheery, and their physical state improved. What doctors and surgeons could not do for them this kind of torture did.

All this while the aged Bishop of Lyons had been lying on his death-bed. He was between 90 and 100 years old, and is said to have been the last surviving disciple of St. John the Divine. It struck the heathen that old Pothinus in some hidden way was strengthening his stubborn flock by his magic, and they carried him before the judgment seat. Here was the chief offender in whom indeed they perceived the Arch offender of all, the Christ Himself. It was a short scene. When he heard the gibes of the mob the dying man revived.

" Who is this God of the Christians ? " said the Governor.

" Thou shalt know if thou art worthy," replied the Bishop of Lyons.

The mob were then told that as long as they did not tear him to pieces they might kick him and pelt him as they pleased. The old man was unconscious when he was carried into the prison, where he died in the arms of his flock.

Then a strange thing happened. It had been a rule since the Emperor Trajan's day that if a man denied that he was a Christian he was to be set free, but once more the law was broken at Lyons, and it was decided to punish those who denied the faith for the crimes they had committed while members of the Church. So the lapsed were put into gaol with the faithful to be punished, although much more lightly, for their crimes, for it was thought worse to be a Christian than to be a cannibal, or to practise monstrous vices. And so now by the faithful full of joy lay the lapsed sunk in despair, and then one by one the lapsed recovered themselves, and repented and confessed and prepared themselves for martyrdom.

And now we reach the crisis of the drama, for the public are to be treated to a series of performances in the amphitheatre, the performers being wild beasts and Christians. It was not a huge stadium like Wembley, it was a smaller and more intimate building like the amphitheatre at Verona. Fill such a place with spectators in the holiday dress of the time, stretch over your heads an orange velarium to protect you from the sun, and join the great crowd of witnesses. Maturus and Sanctus were brought in first. Some forty or fifty men armed with scourges lined up, and the martyrs were made to run the gauntlet of the scourges until they were dripping with blood from head to foot. When they had been made thus attractive to the wild beasts these were uncaged upon them to worry them, but not to kill them. While the mauling went on this or that spectator yelled out some subtlety of torture he wished applied. He was always listened to. Each victim was then placed in the red-hot iron chair, and half broiled alive before the world. All the while only one cry was heard. Monotonous and haunting it came from the lips of Sanctus the Deacon, " I am a Christian. I am a Christian. I am a Christian."

Before proceeding further the Governor wrote to the Emperor for directions. The Emperor directed that Roman citizens who persisted in their atheism should be beheaded ; that the others should be scourged to death, and that all who apostatized should be set free. The Governor beheaded the Roman citizens, and before releasing the lapsed, as a mere formality, ordered them to apostatize again. To his amazement they almost all confessed Christ. He then sent the whole lot to the beasts at the next festival in the amphitheatre. There was a very distinguished citizen named Attalus, for the blood of whom the popular clamour was so great that the Governor could not resist it, and he sent Attalus, Roman citizen as he was, to the beasts and the iron chair. While he was being roasted alive in public, Attalus kept calling out cheerily, " You call us cannibals. We do not eat men. It is you who eat men. You are eating me now." So group after group were despatched until it grew monotonous, and the audience began to look forward to the crowning sensation.

Among the confessors was a boy of fifteen, a young gentleman; a Wykehamist or Etonian of good birth might be his parallel to-day, not quite so sturdy perhaps as they are, for the well-brought-up lads of the second century led very carefully-guarded lives in the beautiful country houses of that day. *The Life of Lord Montagu of Beaulieu* gives a delightful picture of such a boy's life to-day. I am sure John Montagu would have played the part of Ponticus, but I doubt Ponticus being so sturdy as he. This lad, graceful and distinguished, was paired off with poor little Blandina, the shrunken little waif of the slave quarters.

Together they were to be the *bonne bouche* of the festival. Ponticus had been brought in day after day to see all the details of the torture, but not a finger had been laid on him, and each time he had been told that if he said " I am not a Christian " he would be set free. But Ponticus said never a word. At last the moment of testing came. On a cross in the arena Blandina, the slave girl, was strung up in chains, and before her they tortured the boy. To Ponticus all day long Blandina shouted encouragements from her cross to the satisfaction of the audience, who saw that it pro-longed the endurance of Ponticus, whose sufferings were so delightful to behold.

Through the long day Ponticus held on, and then

as sunset approached his young body wilted and collapsed, and his young spirit ascended into the highest heaven.

Blandina's work was done.

"And so," says the Epistle of the Churches of Lyons and Vienne, "the blessed Blandina, last of all, like a mother of high degree, after encouraging her children and sending them before her as conquerors into the presence of the King, making all their conflicts her own, hastened to join her sons and daughters."

It was a senseless body which the heathens took down from the cross and flung to a bull to be gored. Blandina had lifted Ponticus to the portals of heaven, and then Ponticus had taken Blandina unto God.

All through this dreadful story we have heard only one cry, "I am a Christian." It moves each of us to ask himself the question, "Am I a Christian?"

It is a solemn thought that most of my readers would be ready to share the fate of these people if the call came.

In the floor of our sanctuary we have carved in brass the names of our choir-boys who fifteen years ago gave their lives for Britain. You who read this would, I believe, do as much for Christ.

Live worthy of the Martyrs you would be if the call came.

PHOCAS

Let us go and do sacrifice unto the Lord.

Exodus v. 17.

THE *Church Times* heads the leading article of one of its most remarkable numbers with the query " And now ? "

In reply it invites the Bishops to take fresh courage as the true leaders of English Catholicism, it lays stress on the growing strength of Communism and Fascism, two forms of a dominance over the individual which threaten the claims of human personality, it marks the part which youthful enthusiasm has taken in the celebrations of the Centenary of the Oxford Movement, and says we must bring down this enthusiasm to practical issues. But it adds, " Above all, the world needs to see that English Catholics understand self-sacrifice."

Self-sacrifice ! Each of us has got his ideal of conduct, and each one of us is conscious that he himself falls short of it. We do not make good progress with our prayers. We are wanting in definite purpose and perseverance about our life with God and our mission among men. We fail to subdue what the theologians call our irritable appetites, we suffer from irritability, and are apt to be inconsiderate and impatient.

What causes this obstinate gap between our ideal and what we make of it? Why are we not making more effort? It is very depressing that so many people who never commit any scandalous sins and who, in examining their consciences, find very little that is definite to accuse themselves of, still remain so unattractive and uninspiring, with as few definite beauties as definite faults. One fault which they have discovered explains the dreary level they maintain. They are selfish.

Selfishness is the root of all evil, not only of all mortal sin but of all venial sin. Behind prayer-lessness, sloth and irritability, lies selfishness. There is only one impulse which is certain to lead us into the life of prayer, into the life of obedience, into the life of loving patience, and keep us steady in our progress therein. It is not " unselfishness," which appears to me to be the most negative of all negative words, it is self-sacrifice.

What is self-sacrifice?

Self-sacrifice is giving oneself entirely to fulfil the vocation with which God has brought each of us into existence; living for the whole of which one is a tiny part, setting oneself to fulfil that part, as it is possible to do by the help of God's grace, and therefore, since human life here is disordered, suffering, suffering.

One reason why modern English Christians are depressed is that they are leaving out of their beliefs the Fall of Man. Pelagianism has always been the British heresy. The heresy of Pelagius was the notion that its perverse use of free-will has not disordered and degraded the race, that sin can always be cleaned away, leaving the nature in which it has shown itself unaffected, in the same way in which one can clean the tea-leaves out of a china cup. Britons have never taken kindly to the Christian account of sin, and many people to-day think that the theory of physical evolution has finally disposed of it; this is not so.

The Book of Genesis does not state, and the Catholic religion does not assert, that man was created perfect. It asserts that man was created on right lines, that is all. The Bible is the history of the spiritual evolution of man. It is a progressive book from start to finish, and always places man's golden age in the future. But it teaches that man's line of spiritual development has not been the best possible, that he might have had a nobler spiritual history; that it is his own fault that he has not, and, that being the case, that those who would seek the highest find themselves in conflict, not only with much that surrounds them, but also with much that they have inherited, and therefore they suffer accordingly. That is a cheerful doctrine because it is a true one. It reminds me that I inherit a tendency to get out of harmony with God's design, and to use created things not for the end for which they were created.

You and I are spiritually out of sorts, and the pursuit of perfection therefore hurts.

In one way or another everything in this life hurts. Vice hurts—the gradual changes in a vicious face shows that; remedies hurt as disease hurts, and virtue hurts too. "If any man will come after Me," says our Lord, " let him deny himself and take up his cross and follow Me." Our Lord does not mean that His way is the only way of pain, He means that this is the sort of pain His way involves. The service of Satan leads to misery, madness and death. The service of Christ leads to Paradise, but it leads there through suffering of another sort, through the pressure of sin, of misfortune, through agonizing temptation, through loss and persecution, through pain and through death.

But through all these the faithful Christian gives " a reasonable holy and lively sacrifice " unto God, enduring them not because they are in themselves pleasing to God, but because under the conditions of a fallen world some share of them falls on all who serve God faithfully, and enduring them serenely because " many waters cannot quench love, neither can the floods drown it."

It would be a great pity to dwell in a melancholy manner on the sufferings life involves. Life involves suffering however one passes it, but it has also great happinesses, great joys, and should be lived merrily by all determined to fulfil the vocation with which God has brought us into existence, living for the whole of which one is a tiny part : that is the life of self-sacrifice.

The life of self-sacrifice is a merry life. As I say that, the face of a priest I know rises before me, who, I believe, is never for an instant out of pain, but who is never for an instant without a jolly smile.

In reply to the query of the *Church Times*, " And now ? " I answer, " And now an army, please, of such people."

A great many of us know St. Mark's Church in Venice. The mosaics in the vestibule represent Old Testament types and figures, and martyrs with the symbols of their martyrdoms. Among the martyrs in the vestibule is the figure of St. Phocas with the gardener's ladder, a figure rare in art. Phocas lived in Pontus in the third Century. He felt himself called, in face of the awful wickedness of the times, to exhibit the power of the spirit over the flesh in the life of retirement and prayer. Round his hermitage he had planted a beautiful garden. Part of its produce he gave to the poor, and part of it furnished the hospitality which his cottage offered to passing travellers. He himself found his joy and refreshment in worshipping God among the unspoiled things of creation, the roses, the lilies and the violets of his garden.

One evening two strangers knocked at his door. "In the Emperor's name," they said. "We are state officials sent in search of a denounced Christian, one Phocas. His case is clear and decided. We are ordered to search him out and give him the opportunity of recanting. If he refuses we must put him to death. Do you know of such a person?"

Phocas reflected for a moment. "Yes," he said, "I know him, but it is late; rest in my house to-night. To-morrow I will show him to you."

After supper, when his guests were gone to rest, Phocas went out into the moonlit garden where the scent of his flowers lay strong. He moved slowly from flower to flower, touching one and another gently, absorbed in thought.

Then he took a spade, and marking out a certain space among the roses, began to dig. All night he worked, deepening and widening his trench, and when the dawn came the light fell upon a new-made grave into which the roses looked.

Then Phocas returned to his house, and when he had bathed himself he prepared breakfast for his guests. So they all ate and drank. After breakfast their host rose from the table. " To-day," he said, " I promised to show you Phocas. You have not far to seek. I am he. I am ready to suffer in my Master's cause."

There was a great silence. The officers were greatly moved. " This is a hard task for us, sir," they said, " but we have no choice, we must obey the Emperor."

So Phocas led them out into the garden and they killed him, kneeling beside his grave, and when they had laid his body therein, and filled the trench, they took great pains to make the spot as seemly as they could, for they were very sore at heart. Then they went away. So the body of Phocas lay among the roses and his spirit went to God.

This is the Christian spirit of self-sacrifice. It takes the rough with the smooth in the Christian life in this simple way. Its motive is the love which has seen the vision of God in the face of Jesus Christ, the love which says to the temptation to flee from suffering what it says in face of the temptation to sinful pleasure, " How can I do this thing and sin against God ? "

It is the spirit of self-sacrifice combining a cheerful endurance of suffering with cool, deliberate, romantic courage ; and it simply means giving oneself entirely to God for the purpose for which one was created.

The story of Phocas has many points of contact with the orderly beneficent lives of many people, the kindness, the hospitality, the flowers in the garden.

But we are not serving with Christ in his Passion if we are unmindful of the terrible events in the world outside. The self-sacrifice of Phocas was not sufficiently shown by his life of chastity, by his hospitality, by his kindness to the poor. These might have been according to the natural inclinations of a refined and sensitive nature. What lay beneath this simple life was not revealed until the night those terrible strangers came knocking at the door. We have often to ask ourselves whether our lives are really lives of self-sacrifice, because an exceedingly polite, well-mannered selfishness looks uncommonly like self-sacrifice.

And now ?

First, each one of us must enrol once more in the army of Christ crucified.

CONSTANTINE

TWENTY-ONE years ago we celebrated with thanksgiving the Sixteenth Centenary of the toleration of the Church by the World. It was a great step in the return of mankind to God, and in this chapter I am going to sketch the personality of the man who effected it, the Emperor Constantine.

We see him first on a great occasion. It is the 1st of May, 305. An immense concourse has assembled on an open-air durbar ground near Nicomedia to witness the ceremony of the abdication of the Emperor Diocletian, then at the zenith of his power and fame. In the group surrounding the central figure stands a young officer of the army, the son of the junior Emperor of the West, superbly handsome, with a splendid look of swiftness and power about him, a prince of romance, Constantine.

You must remember that the empire had nearly fallen into ruin forty years before this time. Diocletian was the strong man who ultimately saved it. In character he was a pagan Oliver Cromwell. He raised the efficiency of the government by decentralizing it. Rome ceased to count. He appointed Maximian to rule the West while he ruled the East, and he created two junior Emperors who were to replace the seniors after twenty years—Constantius under Maximian, Galerius under himself. Now the twenty years was up, and with solemnity and dignity the senior Emperors were retiring, and Constantius and Galerius were replacing them with two new juniors—Severus in the West, and Maximin in the East.

It must have been by a special providence that Constantine was not assassinated in his youth. He was so obviously made and marked out for greatness. Diocletian had kept him tied to his palace, and now when Diocletian retired, Constantine struggled to get away from the jealous and sullen Galerius. When at last he extracted a permission to visit his father, the young man fled on the instant from the palace. There is a thrilling story of his flight across Europe, killing all the horses at the posting stations to prevent pursuit. He found his father Constantius, the western colleague of Galerius, at Boulogne, and together they crossed to Britain. The splendid young prince became the idol of the army, and when, after a while, Constantius died at York, the soldiers proclaimed Constantine senior Emperor of the West.

There is another exciting story of Constantine refusing the crown, and galloping furiously across the Yorkshire wolds pursued by his adoring soldiers, who tried to fling the imperial mantle over the Prince's head as he galloped before them. Constantine was far too wise to accept the crown and upset the existing system of government, which provided that the junior Emperor should succeed the senior; so Severus succeeded Constantius, and Constantine was made junior Emperor of the West. He soon had all the Gallic provinces at his feet; he was splendidly generous, and a great soldier; and he was strong with the unusual strength of chastity. It was, I think, his natural chastity which made him accessible to Christian influence. Then began the tangle of politics and wars, which ended in Constantine's conversion and supremacy.

Rome, as I have said, had ceased to count, but now Maxentius, son of the retired Western Emperor Maximian, overthrew Severus, usurped the throne, established himself in Rome, and began a Roman renaissance. He revived all the great associations, he invoked the gods of Rome, and he summoned all the powers of black magic to help him. For some time he held the position. Meanwhile Galerius, the senior Eastern Emperor, died horribly, like Henry VIII, and was succeeded by Licinius. Then Maximin, the junior Eastern Emperor, challenged the supremacy of Licinius, and divided the East with him; so that there came a moment when the empire was partitioned into four quarters;

then Constantine and Licinius combined against Maxentius and Maximin. But in the contest which followed, Licinius and Maximin neutralized one another—they paired and did not move—and the great game was played between Constantine sweeping down from Gaul upon the usurping Maxentius standing his ground before Rome.

It was the fine flower of Paganism pitted against all that was worst in it. And Maxentius had the gods of Rome on his side ; he was up to his elbows in magic ; behind him, not metaphorically but literally, stood the prince of this world and his armies. All the auspices forbade Constantine to move, all his generals told him he was going to destruction, for he had to leave half the army to defend the frontiers, and he had only half his opponent's men. It was Constantine against the world. It was Constantine against the gods. The gods ! For how long, thought Constantine, have the Emperors invoked the gods, and how wretchedly most of them have ended. And then Constantius, his father, rose before his mind : noble Constantius, who had worshipped only one God, the God who stands behind the gods—the *divinitas* of the cultured Roman. Constantius, he had lived and died in blessed peace. But who was this God of Constantius ?

Do you see the Emperor ? He is no sinner

seeking a saviour. He is a great general and statesman, with the power of victory burning in his veins,
to whom the inspiration has come that the Roman
world needed a stronger spiritual force than any
it knew. A stronger spiritual force! The Christians! There were now 9,000,000 of them in an
empire of 100,000,000. They were the proclaimed
enemies of the whole point of view of the Roman
world, of its customs, of its pleasures, of its arts;
by their rejection of the religion of the army, by
the anti-social character of their asceticism, by the
strength of their close and largely secret organization, they had been intractable to Diocletian's
master-plan for the rejuvenescence of the empire.
Diocletian and Galerius had tried to destroy them;
they had failed, and lately Galerius in his hideous
living death had cried to them to forgive him and
pray for him. The Christians, a stronger spiritual
force than the Empire knew. What were those
stories of their dauntless courage?

Secunda! Who was Secunda?

She was a little girl of twelve. When her
friends were taken before the Prefect Secunda
insisted on going with them. In vain Christians
and heathen bade her run away and play. Secunda
stood firm. At length, this obstinate Christian of
twelve was condemned to the arena, and the
populace assembled to see her torn to pieces.

Undauntedly Secunda advanced across the arena to meet an immense she-bear. Then a remarkable thing happened. Mr. Bernard Shaw would say that the bear was disappointed at the size of Secunda and thought that if she waited for the next Christian she might get a more adequate luncheon. We should wish to credit the animal with the holy impulse with which she is credited in the Acts of the Martyrs. But history does not analyse the motives of the bear. It only tells us that she lay down at Secunda's feet. So they beheaded Secunda, and with one swift painless stroke sent her to our Blessed Lord.

The Christians !

" O God of Constantius, my father," cried the Emperor, " declare yourself who you are."

And our Lord Jesus Christ broke the silence of the heavens and spoke. There is no doubt about Constantine's vision of the Cross. There is no doubt that to him, as to Saul of Tarsus, there came a message out of the silence, " I am Jesus Whom thou persecutest, it is hard for thee to kick against the pricks." We may pull Eusebius' story to pieces if we please, but there is no doubt of the spiritual experience which comes down to us in the symbolic figures of that narrative. There is no doubt that then and there Constantine was for ever convinced of the truth of the Catholic Faith, and that then and there he placed the Sacred Monogram on his standards. And so with his wonderful power of forced marches he whirled down from the Alps, shattered Maxentius and his forces at the Milvian bridge, and carried up the Cross of Jesus into the Palace of the Cæsars.

The famous Edict of Toleration was issued soon after from Milan. It is a curious undenominational document, because the Eastern Emperor, Licinius, was a pagan. Indeed, the Edict of Milan embodies the religion which the Broad Church party and the Dissenters would like to impose by law upon the people of England.

But such a coalition could not last. The Christians in the dominions of Licinius looked with passionate eagerness towards Constantine. Licinius, the pagan, recognized that there could be no concord between Belial and Christ, and when at last the outstanding disputes between East and West were put to the arbitrament of the sword, Licinius, who had signed the Edict of Milan but who had begun to persecute once more, swore that if the gods gave him victory he would extirpate Christianity from the earth. This last war was frankly between Christian and pagan, and Licinius perished. Once more a single Emperor reigned through East and West, and he had crowned his standards with the symbol of the Cross.

Constantine gave to our Lord everything except himself, and the rest of his story is the story of such a man.

He was cultured, strong and generous, and he had splendid common sense. All these qualities shone in his treatment of the Donatists. Donatism was a Puritan schism on questions of strictness of morals. Constantine's healthy common sense saw the sanity of the Catholic position in the matter, and he was strongly on the Catholic side. His point of view was typical of the average layman of all time. He felt strongly on this practical matter which was only of passing importance, for Donatism had no element of permanence in it, and he never understood or saw the importance of the Arian controversy, which dealt with a point absolutely vital to the continuance of the Christian Religion.

But he was a noble figure at the Council of Nicæa—magnificent, modest and sensible. Many Bishops had sent him complaints about fellow Bishops, and in one of the great scenes of history the Emperor called for a live brazier and then, unfolding his toga, displayed the bundle of scrolls. "These seals have not been broken," said the Emperor, and amid an awful silence, he flung the scrolls into the fire. Then he looked up and said to the Bishops, " Christ begs him who hopes for forgiveness to forgive his erring brother."

But Constantine had never given himself—he was the patron of the Church but still not a Christian ; and a fall came so terrible that I do not hesitate to put it down to the devil and his angels. He went to Rome to celebrate the twentieth year of his reign. Rome was still fiercely pagan, and there amid the haunted chambers of the Palace black terrors began to beset him. Twenty years was Diocletian's limit for an Emperor's reign. If he died now the pagan cause would triumph. Why should not paganism slay him and revive ? The principalities and powers pressed more fiercely upon him with their black temptations. Crispus, his son, was the favourite of the pagans. Fausta, his second wife, had she been faithful to him ? The world was full of plots against him, the corridors full of assassins lurking for the champion of the Church. Crispus was banished, and died. Fausta died, too, and the mystery of her death was never solved. I do not doubt that the Emperor was possessed, and that this was the revenge of the dæmons who were the gods of Rome.

When the cloud lifted, the remorse was life-long.

He could never bear to live in Rome again, and he built Constantinople. He tried to forget in building ; he lavished buildings and riches on the Churches. Had he been in the hands of an Ambrose he might have made a great repentance before the world, but he was in the hands of Eusebius of Nicomedia, the friend of Arius, who was singularly like the latitudinarian Bishops of our eighteenth century, a sort of Bishop Hoadly. Personal religion was not the forte of Eusebius of Nicomedia. The Empress Helena went on pilgrimage to the Holy Places, the sepulchre of the Lord was uncovered, the Church of the Anastasis arose.

But in his failure to advance, the Emperor degenerated. Eutropius says that his earlier years were those of the greatest of princes, his latter years those of an average prince. He grew weary of the burden of affairs ; he divided his sovereignty among his sons, but his soul found no rest.

In the thirtieth year of his reign the world hailed him as the Emperor who had reigned longer than any since Augustus. That year the Church of the Anastasis at Jerusalem was consecrated, and it became clear to the Emperor that his end was not far off.

In justice we must remember that so far he had postponed Baptism from a profound sense of its obligations, and an uncertainty whether a man in his position could submit to all the demands of our Lord. Now he knew that for him the Lord was at hand. In the Church of St. Lucian the Martyr at Helenopolis, kneeling in the centre of the Nave, the

Emperor confessed his sins before the Church, and was admitted a catechumen. Then to the Palace of Nicomedia he summoned all the Bishops of the neighbourhood, and before a great assemblage he made his profession of Faith. The supreme moment had come—he laid aside the Imperial purple and descended into the saving flood which was at once his grave and his mother. He was baptized and pardoned by the Precious Blood, and they robed him in the white robe of Baptism—the Imperial purple he refused ever to touch again. A white bed had been prepared, and on it they laid the white Emperor, the new-born child of the Church.

So he lay until he died. His captains came to bid him farewell, and at the awe-inspiring sight they broke down and wept, but the Emperor spoke cheerily. "I have only one wish now," he said, "I have won pardon and peace. I only seek to hasten my journey to God."

He died on the 22nd of May, 337.

It is a chequered story, the tragedy of which touches out hearts. It leaves a plain lesson in our minds. No amount of interest in the Church, advocacy of her claims, championship of her rights— no self-sacrifice, no generosity, no time, no trouble of laborious days, in the cause of Christ—can save a man from his sins and secure his salvation. One thing only can do that, the Precious Blood of Christ, sought in Baptism, in Penance, and at the Altar, with the penitence and faith of a little child.

THE LIFE AND DEATH OF ST.
JOHN CHRYSOSTOM

TWO hundred years have passed since that
day in the amphitheatre of Lyons when the
spirits of Ponticus and Blandina entered into the
joy of their Lord. The Empire, divided now
into West and East, and with a new capital, Constantinople, is nominally Christian. Theodosius,
the last great Roman Emperor, is reigning with
the inefficient help of his weak sons, Honorius
and Arcadius. Two great saints arise and live in
West and East during a period of religious and
political confusion. The Western Saint—Ambrose
of Milan—I tried to show some years ago,[1]
now I am attempting a lightning sketch of the
Eastern Saint, John of Antioch, whom men called
Chrysostom—John of the Golden Mouth.

It was a critical moment in the age-long battle
of Catholic Christians, the battle for no compromise
with the world in matters of Christian faith and
morals. Arianism, the contention that Christ was
just a little less than God, was really Paganism
elegantly disguised, and it revealed this no less

[1] *Saints and Leaders.*

by its spirit than by its doctrine. If Arianism had triumphed, Christianity would have perished, and Ambrose the Bishop was fighting the battle against Arianism from his throne at Milan. The fight for Christian morals was a more difficult one, for at this moment the majority of Christians were only Christians in name, and had definite pagan ideas and customs which they refused to give up. Living with them in equality of opportunity were the Faithful of Christian ancestry, preserving the sacred tradition of the Christian life which traced back to Pentecost. It seemed an intolerable position. The Faithful felt like the descendants of some noble family whose palace, made sacred by a hundred memories, had been taken possession of by a gang of disreputable strangers. Out of the misery of this a good emerged, and Religious Vocations were developed on a great scale. Large religious communities and multitudes of solitaries arose on all sides seeking to save the purity of the Church by unceasing prayer and the example of complete chastity, poverty and obedience. But connected with this there was a danger. Good, invertebrate people felt that they would like to live in and about the religious communities without being of them. They shrank from contact with their half-pagan fellow Christians, and wished to keep themselves to themselves and know nothing of their neighbours. This was of course no remedy. This was as far as possible from being like Christ. There were only two ways of helping. Prayer with Christ on the high mountain apart, or work with Christ in the midst of the crowd. You could not help by living apart, half-way up the hill.

Then there arose a man who did both, who came down from the high mountain apart and worked for the devil-wracked mob in the plain. It killed him, but he did it. When at length they brought his dead body back to Constantinople, from which he had been expelled, the young Emperor lay weeping, his wet cheek pressed to the coffin lid.

Listen then to a drama not so much of external happenings as of the interior life. Listen to this tale of John of Antioch, surnamed Chrysostom, John of the Golden Mouth.

In about the year 347 there was born at Antioch, to Secundus, one of eight Field Marshals of the Imperial army, and his wife, the lady Anthusa, a son, a very small son, whom they named John. John was a tiny, delicate thing, who had to be kept in cotton-wool. Later on he was found to be a very clever little boy; he was given the Eton and Trinity College, Cambridge, education of those days, which was entirely pagan.

John completed his intellectual training under the great pagan philosopher, Libanius. When Libanius was asked whom he considered to have been his best pupil, he used to say, " John, if the Christians had not stolen him from us." John was pale and thin, hollow-cheeked, with big luminous eyes below a broad forehead. He lost his masses of soft hair in middle age, and became bald, bent and shrunken. It was a frail scabbard which the sword of the spirit wore out. He was not baptized until he was grown up, but he went through no period of youthful excess like Augustine, and was the treasure of his devout Christian mother Anthusa.

From the first John wanted to be an ascetic of the desert. That was the ideal which inspired him. He thought of it as boys to-day think of flying, wireless, and speed records. He yearned for a great adventure in the spiritual world as a man may yearn to-day for a great adventure across the Arabian desert, above the habitable atmosphere, or under the Arctic ice, but his mother always said " No." She saw that he was physically unfit, and she also saw his amazing sympathy for all things human, and felt that if he could be brought into close contact with the crowd he might do wonders for the cause of our Lord.

So John, who was baptized when he reached

the age of twenty-one, lived the life of a good layman in the big house at Antioch, much influenced by the worthy bishop, Meletius, and by a devoted friend called Basil. Suddenly, in the funny way of the Church of those days, they tried to force him to become a bishop, and John escaped into the mountains, entered a religious community, and was lost to the world. Three or four years later he went further, and for two years lived the life of a solitary in a cave in the hills. Then his health gave way, for Anthusa was right. John's body was not designed for this, it was designed for something else. " I must not kill myself," he said, " this collapse shows that I am meant to live in the world and minister to it," so he went back to Antioch, and was ordained priest by Bishop Flavian, who made him missioner of the diocese.

Antioch was still what it had been in the days of St. Paul. It was still, to quote Renan's phrase, " a stream of wild pleasure, delicately conceived, daintily dressed." An excitable, feverish place; now, thanks to its Christian leaven, full of the wildest inconsistencies. Here in the enormous golden church built by Constantine, and in the Palaia, the older, simpler church, held to stand on ground blessed by the feet of Peter and Paul, John began to preach the greatest sermons in history.

See the great golden church packed to over-flowing day after day by the half pagan people who so scandalized the faithful of the old régime. John's slight, small figure is standing at the lectern. He never used the pulpit because he said he felt nearer to the people at the lectern. And in this lies the secret of his attractiveness. John's secret was the greatest of all. He loved each of his hearers as God loved him, not for the virtues the man shared with others, but for what was peculiar to that man and unlike all others. Each of us is unique, and it was that uniqueness which John loved. You see? God has given to each of us a distinctive mark, and John loved this distinctive mark as God loves it. These distinctive marks which distinguish A from B, and C from D, are, of course, the raw materials which make the diversities of life. John loved persons, ranks, classes, callings, societies, as things divine in their origin, like mountains, lakes, forests, flowers and seas. This means that he touched human life at every point. No, there was never such a preacher as John. What was the thing that struck men about John? It was his sunshine, his vigour, his elasticity. Newman says that John Chrysostom was the personification of a day in Spring, showery, sunny, and glittering through its rain. It was his love for each that made John's sermons so exciting.

It enabled him to dispense with tact. We treat a congregation gingerly, like a dog which has to be handled carefully. John used his knife, when it had to be used, like a great surgeon. I think it must have been the " Sermons on the Statues " which completed his conquest of Antioch. The people had broken out into a violent riot, and had thrown down the Imperial Statues. For months they lived in expectation of the destruction of the city and the extirpation of its inhabitants. During that time John did not exhort the city or rebuke the city, he stood in the midst of it, embodying its penitence, and feeling its grief in every fibre of his being. Can there be greater preaching than that ? The Imperial Court had never seen before what a great asset in government extraordinary sanctity can be, and Antioch was spared.

Ten years passed, and the ten years confirmed the Government in its high opinion of Chrysostom's power over people. So when Nectarius, the wealthy, genial, and easy-going Bishop of Constantinople, died, Eutropius, the exceedingly unattractive Lord Chamberlain of the Emperor, determined to kidnap John and force him to become Bishop of Constantinople. One day the Governor of Antioch invited John to drive with him into the country. Outside the city the Imperial guards arrested him and carried him post-

haste to Constantinople, where he was commanded
to accept the Bishopric. It was just a little bit
more irregular than our *congé d'élire*.

Eutropius, who was practical ruler of the Eastern
Empire, had kidnapped John to help him govern.
John read the thing differently, " Come and carry out
the reforms in Christian morals you have preached.
You have preached a revival of the purity of the
Apostolic Church, come to the Throne of Constantinople and revive it." So John said, " I will." As
always, he trusted to simplicity and love and not to
tact. Now tact is needed to avoid the Cross in life.

Suppose that on the death of Archbishop Benson,
Lord Salisbury had forcibly made Arthur Stanton
Archbishop of Canterbury, I feel sure that Arthur
Stanton would have said what John said, " When
you sweep a staircase you must begin at the top,"
and that he would have shut up Lambeth Palace
as John shut up the palace at Constantinople.

But that does not take one very far. It is people,
not things, that count. John had the World to
fight in his patron Eutropius, the Flesh in the
beautiful Empress Eudoxia, a Byzantine Catherine
of Russia, and the Devil in his spiritual superior,
Theophilus, the Patriarch of Alexandria. John
had disappointed Eutropius, who became his first
enemy. When Eutropius fell from power John
tried to get justice and mercy for him, but Eutropius

83

was killed and Eudoxia became the power behind the throne. A magnificent and lovely pagan in Christian clothes, Eudoxia for a time was captivated by John, and led the adoring crowds who surrounded his pulpit, but after a while she felt that John was reading the secrets of her heart, and her admiration became resentment. This flamed into hatred when John denounced the pagan festivities at the unveiling of the silver statue of the Empress set up before the cathedral. An offended woman makes a bad enemy for a priest; an affronted empress makes a worse enemy for a bishop, and Eudoxia, knowing that John was trying to reform the morals of the clergy, conspired with the Patriarch of Alexandria to get him removed. It took some three years to remove him, and another three to kill him by natural means, because no one would use poison or violence, but in the end it was done. They tried John for technical irregularities in a synod packed with his ecclesiastical enemies. John refused to plead, appear, or take notice of the verdict. He took the attitude we Anglo-Catholics have always taken about our packed trials and their foregone conclusions. Indeed, Father Mackonochie's death in the forest of Mamore, except that it was not deliberately planned, was, in effect, a modern parallel to Bishop John's death in the shrine of Basiliscus.

The Church John tried to reform drove him
into exile, and harried him in exile until he died.
There was a moment when if he had dropped a
spark among the adoring laity he might have
seized the city and overturned the throne, but the
follower of our Lord could not do that. So he
hid himself and slipped away silently from the
scene.

Do you realize that exile lost half its terrors
when men learned that the world was round?
In John's day the world was a flat plane with a
brilliantly-lighted centre, from which you could
apparently be taken right off the map into unknown
desolation. Knowing John's sensitiveness Eudoxia
ordered him as far as possible off the map. The
idea was to carry him across Asia Minor towards
the Caucasus until he died. For years John's
health had been terribly bad; he appears to have
suffered from almost chronic colitis and violent
attacks of recurring fever. He could not eat
ordinary food, and any extreme of heat or cold
brought on an illness. The worst climate pro-
curable was on the confines of Armenia, and John
could not bear any rough movements because of
his colitis, so the plan was to carry him thither
on a palanquin slung between two mules under a
guard ordered to keep him moving as much as
possible. His enemies were greatly aided in their

plans for him by the Isaurian bandits, the pre-
decessors of the Kurds, who, in the same regions
and in our own day, have extirpated under Turkish
auspices the Christian Armenians. John and his
party were delivered from the monotony of travel
by having to spend weeks and months playing
hide and seek with Isaurian bandits. The bishops
through whose dioceses he passed were ordered
to hurry him on. Once when he was very danger-
ously ill a good lady took him into her country
house. In the middle of the night a neighbouring
priest aroused him in great excitement and told
him that the Isaurians were coming and would
massacre the party. He was got out of bed, put
into the carrying chair, and ordered forward up
a mountain pass. No torches were allowed.
Then one of the mules stumbled in the darkness,
overturned the *lectica*, and flung the bishop into
the road. The priest dragged him to his feet and
urged him forward, and he staggered on for hours
up a stony track in pitch darkness. It is most
pathetic that in the letters he wrote to his best
friends he made the best he possibly could of his
condition, his situation was always " greatly improved," his health which had been so bad was
" now re-established " ; to correspondents who
would not grieve so much he sketched the other
side of the picture.

86

But John was tougher than his enemies hoped, and in the third winter of his exile his health grew better. So it was determined to bring matters to a close. A fresh guard was chosen and told to take him by forced marches to the eastern shores of the Black Sea. He stood three months of this increased torture, then collapsed and died near a place called Comana in Pontus.

And this is how he died. He was very near death when they came to Comana, and he asked the guards to halt there, but they dragged him some miles farther to a place called Arabissus, where the night was passed. Again next day he asked the guards to halt since his illness was so severe, but they would not, and marched on some miles past the little chapel of the martyr Basiliscus, which stood outside the village. Then one of them looked into the carrying chair, and saw in the shrunken face of Chrysostom that at last the change had come, and that the end was at hand. It was useless to go farther with a dead body, so they carried him back to the martyr's chapel.

Those of you who know St. David's have been in such chapels; the martyry of Basiliscus was a small oblong building of stone, with a slab of stone for an altar, like St. Justinian's chapel on Ramsey Sound.

Into the empty building the guards carried the

Bishop's chair, pulled out the poles, and left him
alone with two or three attendants. The Bishop
made a little gesture towards his heart, and an
attendant pulled back the many wrappings in
which he was travelling and took out a small
silver phial. He dusted the stone slab and set
the phial down. It contained the Most Holy
Viaticum. Then the Bishop pointed towards a
little valise which always travelled with him.
They unwrapped it and uncovered a pile of pure
white linen—they were John's baptismal robes.
Made for a young man of twenty, they were rather
large for him now. The Bishop pointed to his
travelling clothes. "Divide these among yourselves," he whispered, and they took off all his
clothes, washed his body with water, and robed
him from head to foot in the pure white linen.
Then one brought to him the silver phial, and he
received his last communion.

They knelt behind him, keeping silence, and
left him sitting alone before the altar, robed in
white. After a while he moved and spoke,
"Glory be to God for all things," said the Bishop.
The silence which followed was not broken.

The golden mouth had spoken for the last time.

ST. EDWARD THE CONFESSOR

And Jesus called a little child unto Him, and set him in the midst of them.

Matthew xviii. 18.

THE Feast of the Translation of St. Edward the Confessor commemorates the day when in the reign of Henry III his relics were placed in the shrine where they still rest.

Let us remember now the Confessor and the building of his Church.

Think of the earliest London. It stood entrenched on Tower Hill, Cornhill and Ludgate Hill; before it ran the river which gave it its existence; behind it lay marshes still remembered in Finsbury, Fenchurch and Moorfields; and behind the marshes rose the fearful forests of Hampstead and Highgate, full of wild bulls, red deer and wild boar. Swift streams ran from the hills to the river. The Walbrook was dangerous in winter flood. The Holburne, or the brook in the hollow, became a stream of sacred wells; there were St. Clement's Well and the Holy Well near the Strand of the river, and farther north there was the Clerkenwell. Here, west of London, the river itself had several channels fed by streams from the north. One, the Eye, the Eyebourne or brook, or Tyburn, ran down from Hampstead and wound under Aye Hill—Hay Hill we Cockneys call it now—and meandered on into a marsh where is now the Green Park. There was a clearance on the wooded bank of the burn and in the clearance a little chapel to our Lady, St. Mary by the Burn. St. Marylebone we call it to-day. Beyond the marsh to which the Eyeburn flowed there rose in the middle of the river a big bank of gravel, an island. The island was overgrown with a dense jungle of big trees and thorn bushes, and it was the lair of some of the most dangerous wild beasts of the region ; it appears first in the Chronicle, as the *locus terribilis*, and as such no doubt it figured in the nightmares of little British and Roman boys and girls.

Presently the Romans, with their genius for a good site, partly cleared it and built a temple there. Time passed, and the good King Lucius, who afterwards became a Swiss bishop and whose relics lie to-day in the Cathedral of Coire, turned the temple into a Christian Church. Then in the seventh century King Sebert built a church on this Isle of Thorns, as it was called.

You remember the legend of its consecration. Late one night the fisherman Edric was fishing from the island bank when he saw a bright light where Lambeth Palace now stands. He crossed and found an old man in foreign dress, who desired to be ferried to the island, and when he landed there the air became radiant, the little church which was to be consecrated by the Bishop on the morrow " stood out without darkness or shadow," angels descended with tapers and incense, and the stranger consecrated the building. It was St. Peter; and he bade the fisherman tell the Bishop that the church was consecrated and show him the marks. Next day the Bishop came and Edric met him and " gave a great salmon in a gentle manner from St. Peter to the Bishop." Then he showed the Bishop the consecration crosses and the Bishop was satisfied that St. Peter had hallowed his own church.

Later on St. Dunstan, marking its seclusion and yet nearness to London, its healthy soil, its two fresh springs and the abundance of salmon and other fish in the river around it, planted a group of Benedictines there, and Londoners called the colony the Western Minster. By this time the terrible Isle of Thorns had become a sunny, happy place lying out in the river crowded with ships of merchandise among the green meadows and fruitful fields of the golden period of the Saxon Kingdom—so it lay in the sunshine awaiting King Edward and its destiny.

King Edward! We see him first a lad at the Norman Court, where his youth was spent in exile, during the last of the Danish periods. A slight-limbed and graceful lad with long transparent fingers which afterwards had the gift of healing, a lad with the palest flaxen hair, and such exquisite colouring of rose and snow that the memory of it has come down to us.

Edward was a born mystic; often in gay company he would suddenly grow silent and remote, his eyes fixed on a landscape none could see. Then he would break into a low laugh of which no one shared the secret. To Edward the invisible things were more clearly seen than the visible. A Saxon Aloysius, destined for a rude throne tottering to its fall. He swore two oaths which show his mind. He swore perpetual vir-ginity—for he had come through the dangers of the Norman Court unsmirched by the smallest stain upon his purity. And he swore that if he ever regained his crown he would go on pilgrimage to St. Peter's tomb at Rome.

A bloodless monk you think. Not at all. A great hunter, tireless in the chase, the gayest and most genial of companions, a general who led victorious armies, a statesman who built a great fleet and made a firm peace.

But beyond all, a prophet, a prophet who rightly

ST. EDWARD THE CONFESSOR

judged the tendencies of his time. The day of
Saxon England was over, it was dying of insularity.
Edward threw a bridge across to France and let
in the Continent.

A modern historian has remarked that Edward
saw that the greatest danger to England lies in
that dread of novelty, that dread of ideas which is
written deep into our history. He sums up the
habitual English frame of mind as " complacency
punctuated now and again with panic," and adds
that if the English people had fully responded to
the King they canonized they might have had the
Norman gifts without the Norman Conquest. As
it was, the last of the Saxons was canonized under
the Normans, and that fact shows him to have
been one of the inspired bridge-builders of history.

When he got his crown he prepared to keep his
oath of pilgrimage, but his people said No, the
times were such that the King must stay at home ;
so he bowed to their will and offered God instead
such a church as England had never known. For
remember, Edward's Abbey was far beyond the
needs of the place and the understanding of the
English. It was as big as the present Church,
with a noble monastery attached. The English
had never seen before a cruciform Church with
vaults of stone and rich carvings and windows of
painted glass. The Abbey summed up in the

noblest of symbols all that Edward hoped for England in the years that were coming. It was built in the power of joy and thanksgiving, faith and hope, while the horizon of the future blackened with a tempest, the end of which none could foretell.

He chose the Isle of Thorns because his prophetic instinct told him that it was England's second holy place—Glastonbury was the first. God had conse-crated Sebert's little Church. To it King Edward had one day carried a lame beggar in his arms and had seen him depart cured from the Altar. There he had seen a vision in the Holy Sacrament at sight of which he had laughed his mysterious laugh of happiness and whispered, "It is Jesus Whom I know." So Edward rebuilt the Palace the Kings had used at times, and came and lived in it to watch the rising of the Abbey. For fifteen years the King watched the Abbey grow, and his life there consecrated the Palace to be the sacred centre of the Empire, the fountain of our legislature.

As the Abbey waxed the King waned. Frailer and frailer grew his earthly tabernacle. His hair was snow-white now, and the long fingers that healed were thin and ivory, but in his face there still lingered the rose bloom of his boyhood. At the last Easter banquet, sitting on his throne in his golden crown, they saw him pass into one of his vision states and heard the long, low, mysterious laugh.

He had been to Ephesus, he said when he returned, and had seen the Seven Sleepers turn in their sleep : it forebode great disturbances for the world.

Thinner and thinner grew the veil which hung between the King's two lives—the life here and the life there. He gave a ring to a beggar and the beggar vanished, but far away in Syria two Shropshire men benighted on the mountains met a wonderful old man with a burning torch, who greeted them with joy and led them to a house where he entertained them and set them on their way. He told them that he was St. John the Divine, and he gave them the ring which the King had given to the mysterious beggar, and bade them restore it to him.

Do not think these stories idle tales—Edward was the man of the legends. He was a mystic, a clairvoyant, a prophet and a healer, and as to the other wonders of his legend at least they illustrate some other aspects of his relation to heaven and earth.

Christmas came—the Abbey stood complete and the King came for the consecration. But on Christmas Day God laid His hand on him. He began to fail quickly ; the consecration was post-

poned till the Feast of the Innocents, but the
King could not be there. He made all the arrangements and ordered every detail. To this he gave
his last strength—indeed, Edward died of the
consecration of the Abbey. He died like a King,
rousing himself to sit on his throne in his golden
crown and to smile and to jest while the courtiers
feasted.

Then the end came. Edith, the Queen, sat on
the ground holding in her lap the cold feet of the
Saint with whom she had lived long in virginity
and bedewing them with her tears. After a long
silence the King spoke his last word to Edith,
and through her to all his people and to all the
world. " Weep not," he said, " I go from the
land of the dead to the land of the living."

" And then," says the Chronicler, " St. Peter,
his friend, opened the gate of Paradise and St.
John, his own dear one, led him before the Divine
Majesty."

" It is Jesus Whom I know." That happy
discernment of his Lord in the Holy Sacrament
gives the clue to the life of St. Edward. It was
the literal imitation of our Lord, not in the poverty
of Francis but upon the throne of England, that
he attempted. Our Lord was the love of his life,
and when he said to the scullion who was stealing
his gold, " Make haste and go, for when Hugolin

comes he won't let you keep a halfpenny," it was the Divine paradox of the Sermon on the Mount he had in mind. There is much prudent application of the Sermon on the Mount. It is well that once an English King should act it out with child-like literalness. Edward had great gifts and graces and a prescient mind, but he lies to-day in his shrine at Westminster because he had the heart of a little child. It is a great company that is gathered in our Abbey—Kings and Queens, nobles, statesmen, sailors, soldiers, lawyers, scholars, scientists, painters, poets and actors. What is the magnet which has drawn them there? What brings our sovereigns to be crowned in that Church and sets the Palace of our lawgivers at its gates?

Ah! the magnetic power of our Abbey lies in the fact that there through the ages is perpetuated a lovely scene of long ago.

Jesus has called a little child and set him in the midst.

IT is said the English have been passionately fond of only two men: one was Lord Nelson and the other was Thomas Becket. Nelson fell fighting England's battles; Becket deliberately gave his life for the principle of the freedom and self-government of the Church of Christ.

Becket was an extraordinary man, raised up to assert that age-long antagonism between the world and the Church, which is the theme of the First Epistle of St. John. On October 13th, 1163, St. Thomas pontificated at the translation of the relics of St. Edward to their present shrine in Westminster Abbey; on December 29th, 1170, he was martyred in Canterbury Cathedral. St. Edward the Confessor laid the foundations of the British Empire by breaking down the English insularity. It was he who threw a bridge across the Channel and let in the Continent. The Norman infusion was a necessary ingredient in the greatness of England, but it had the defects of its qualities. Those defects slew St. Thomas.

Thomas Becket was a Londoner, the son of Gilbert and Mathilda Becket. He was born in the

City on the Feast of St. Thomas the Apostle, and he was educated by the Augustinians of Merton Abbey. An athletic Westminster schoolboy has very much the same upbringing to-day. But no Westminster boy has so jolly a time as Thomas had; those were the days of Merrie England. Life was full of strong lights and shadows. There was more sunshine and laughter, and there was more darkness and crying, for the black and white have now become varying shades of grey. Thomas had a glorious time, great aquatic sports on the river, football in the fields, tobogganing, and even a sort of ski-ing in the hard winters; later on in youth, hawking, baiting, and hunting. The curriculum of Merton Abbey would amuse the authorities of modern public schools, but it gave the boys what no modern school can give them— it gave them Latin as a living universal language and so made them citizens of Europe. When Thomas was about seventeen he went to the University of Paris, where he sat under the lecturers and mixed with the men of all nations. Amid this wonderful diversity and richness of experience he lived in the unbroken unity of the one Catholic Faith, and in all the freshness of ardent imaginative youth he got an impression of an age-long Church, the same in all lands, superior to all merely national laws, fortunes and fashions. The loss of this impression through the disruption of the Reformation is no doubt the greatest disaster which has ever befallen the English. When he was twenty-one he came back to London, and went into a City firm—Osborn Wilddenniers and Company, in order to get a good business training.

Thomas was a Peter Pan ; he never grew up in the poor conventional Wendy sense. As he was at twenty-one, so he remained in heart and impulse until his blood and brains lay scattered on the pavement of Canterbury Cathedral. And already at twenty-one it is possible to sketch him. He was enormously tall, broad and long-legged, with strong, thin aquiline features under a broad forehead, and very bright, big eyes rather far apart, He had marvellously developed senses, the eye of a hawk, the ear of a stag, and the scent of a hound. He was a great rider and sportsman. He was the sort of youth who is completely unconscious of popularity ; he was very frank and very courteous, and he was always beautifully dressed. He had an attractive failing—he was very quick-tempered. So far he resembles many gallant and charming young men. How did he differ from them ? First, he had a tremendously magnetic personality ; that of course is a natural endowment ; you found yourself greatly attracted or repelled, you did not know why. Secondly, his psychological instincts

were as highly developed as his physical senses.
He was like the prophet in Samaria who knew
what the King of Israel was thinking about in his
bed-chamber. Thirdly, he was absolutely single-
minded and determined. Now the absolutely
single-minded and determined are the rarest of the
rare. St. John the Divine was one, St. Thomas
of Canterbury was another. For example, he saw
that the law of Christ required virginity for the
unmarried, and so, although he had very strong
passions, he remained virgin, and since he became
an ecclesiastic he remained virgin to the end.
And it was this which won him his martyr's crown.
Thomas was a Samson with whom Delilah failed
altogether. In this life of secret consistency and
virginity, of entire devotion to his Captain Christ,
and of love for Christ's Blessed Mother, his strength
and determination rose greater and greater with
the years, until the world was obliged to slay him
lest he should slay the world.

But in his early days the world was very fond
of him. " Here is a young man," said the world,
" who is bound to rise to the highest place; he
must be given the widest opportunities." Such
opportunities were then best found not in the
English State, but in the Catholic Church. Thomas
was attached to the Court of Archbishop Theobald
of Canterbury, and spent eleven years in the service

of the Archbishop. This meant a great deal of legal work and a good deal of social work too. The Archbishop made him his confidant; it was natural to hand over to him delicate negotiations. Thomas soon saw that his life was to be an ecclesiastical one, and he got leave of absence for a year, and went to Bologna and mastered the Canon law. "A man of transcendent force," everybody said, "the ablest man in England." He made a host of bitter enemies; it was impossible it could be otherwise, as he sailed on towards supreme greatness, not through ambition, but through determination to do perfectly what he had to do, through personal magnetism and immense practical ability. In those days the Archdeacon of Canterbury was Prime Minister of that *imperium in imperio*, the Church in England, and when the Archdeacon Roger Pont l'Eveque, who had found himself replaced in the Archbishop's counsels by a mere secretary, and hated Thomas accordingly, was made Archbishop of York in 1153, Thomas was made Archdeacon of Canterbury, and received deacon's orders for the purpose. He had only been in minor orders before.

A few months after, young Henry II, a lad of twenty-one, was crowned, and next year laid his hand upon the most remarkable of his subjects. Henry had great plans and ambitions, and he took the strongest personality in the kingdom to help him. In 1155, the Archdeacon of Canterbury, the Archbishop's right-hand man, was also made the King's right-hand man and Lord Chancellor of England. Henry was twenty-one, and Thomas was thirty-seven, and Henry adored Thomas with a mad hero-worship. It was a young King Saul and an older David. There was a great deal of King Saul in Henry II. He was an abler king than Saul, but, like Saul, he was loving and fierce and generous and passionate. He was full of fun and jollity, but there were times of ungovernable rage, when he tore the cushions of his couch to pieces and chewed the stuffing. The heroic vein in Henry aroused all the Peter Pan element in Thomas, and the King and the Chancellor fought, governed, and worked like strong soldiers and statesmen, and loved and romped like a pair of schoolboys.

It was the dawn of the English democracy : as towns showed power of self-government they were given charters. These charters curtailed the powers of the nobles. In all his development of the Commonwealth the Chancellor had the worst of the nobles dead against him, and all the poor passionately on his side. So it remained throughout his career ; from birth to death it was true of Thomas as of his Lord and God that the common people heard him gladly. Those were days when kings and chancellors never put off their state except to hunt and to sleep. Thomas, whose motto through life was to do everything completely, kept the most magnificent state as Lord Chancellor of England. He himself ate and drank very sparingly, for his digestion was bad; but for the rest he played his semi-royal part right royally, and his journey as Chancellor to settle the boundaries of the English territories in France was one of the greatest mediæval progresses of which the record has come down. But there was always another side to the Chancellor known only to his confessor and his God. On many nights the state bed was unoccupied and the Chancellor lay on the floor. Often he bared his back to the lash of the discipline, and on many moonless nights a tall figure might have been seen wrapped in a cloak, kneeling through long hours in the cold porch of some locked church absorbed in prayer. Few knew that it was the figure of the Chancellor who kept such princely state.

If Henry had had more sympathy with the religion of his friend the great tragedy would never have happened. He chose to think as little of it as possible, to think of Thomas and himself as being one heart and one soul, whereas all the while Henry was a bad Catholic and Thomas a good one. But together they made a great king; and after old

Archbishop Theobald's death Henry conceived the plan of conquering that *imperium in imperio*, the Church in England, by setting his twin soul on the throne of Augustine. As Chancellor, Thomas had been a relentlessly strong steward of the worldly interests of England. In the blindness of his pride of place and vanity Henry imagined that at his bidding this strong steward would bind the English dioceses to the legs of the English throne. Really it is the most dramatic mistake in history.

The scene is the castle of Falaise in France. The Chancellor, travelling to England to quiet some revolts in Wales, has entered the King's presence in his rich riding-dress to take leave.

" I am going to make you Archbishop, Chancellor."

The eye of a hawk, the ear of a stag, the scent of a hound—the magnificent giant stood still a moment, and his wonderful instinct looked down the perspective of the future right to the end. But he laughed, " Absurd, sir."

" I am going to make you Archbishop, Chancellor."

" Then you will regret it, Sir, to the day of your death."

But as he rode to England he thought it out. He knew what he stood for in the eyes of the King, that this was a scheme for the subjugation of the

Church in England by the world. It was as lord of the world that Henry's nominee was to rule the Church. Thomas thought it out, and he saw that he must accept the Primacy and stand firm for God. How strange it all seems to us! There was a gorgeous progress to Canterbury. On Saturday in Whitsun week the Lord Chancellor was ordained Priest, and on Trinity Sunday he was consecrated Archbishop, said his first Mass, and was enthroned. There was a great banquet, and as the Archbishop left the hall the jesters surrounded him, as they had been accustomed, demanding money and praise. The Archbishop paused and smiled. "I am not the man who was the Chancellor," he said. Gradually he laid aside all his magnificence, until the figure which had kept vigil at the church gates at night stood revealed to the world. We know how he lived at Canterbury. Night after night the Archbishop chanted the night office in his cathedral with the monks; the early dawn he passed in study and meditation; then he served the breakfast of a group of poor persons. He said his Mass at nine, the tears often streaming down his cheeks. At midday he dined in silence, and then took a siesta. Sometimes he rode in the afternoon, sometimes he walked in the cloisters, sometimes he tended the sick in the infirmary. After early supper he said evening prayer with his chaplains, and often received the discipline before lying down, to be roused before long for the night office.

News of the life of the Archbishop reached the King, who laughed an angry laugh. "Thomas is mad," he cried. The enemies of Thomas sneered. "A pose," they said, "a pose. Thomas has always known how to play his part." But the religious and the people knew the truth about the Archbishop, and gave him all their hearts. And as to the genuineness of a great man—*Securus judicat orbis terrarum*.

So we find Thomas Becket on the throne of St. Augustine, set there to subjugate the Church to the world, and determined to guard it for God at the price of his life. His first step was the resignation of the Great Seal. Such an archbishop as he meant to be could not be Lord Chancellor. It was the declaration of war, and the King was angry and aghast. But there were affectionate greetings when the King returned to England, and an external harmony for about a year, during which Henry, puzzled and sullen, gathered all the critics of Thomas around him and began the subjugation of the Church, with the strongest man in Europe on the other side. Henry had not known before how much of his strength was his own and how much was Thomas'; now he knew, and he went in angry fear of being worsted before the people.

They fought the first round at the Council of Westminster. Thomas stood firm, and the King left the hall in silence, his face lurid with anger. Next day the Archbishop was required to give up the estates the King had bestowed upon him, and he gave them up. This thoroughly frightened the Bishops, who felt that disendowment was in the air, and they began to scuttle over to the King. Indeed, the sudden appearance of this tremendous ecclesiastical figure in the defence of the Church frightened every nervous sympathizer; unfortunately the Pope was one of the nervous sympathizers, and it was largely at the Pope's entreaty that Thomas made his one big mistake at the Council of Clarendon. The King was trying to secure his point and get a large control of the Church into his hands, but everyone assured Thomas that he was not doing more than saving his dignity before the nation in the matters under dispute. For the moment Thomas assented, but when he saw the papers he found he had been outwitted, and refused to put his seal to them. His cross-bearer told him the bitter truth: " My lord, you have betrayed your conscience and your good name." The Archbishop burst into tears, and for forty days he refrained from saying Mass. From this moment every sort of persecution was visited on the Archbishop, culminating in the attempt to ruin him by making him personally responsible for sums of money which had passed through his hands as Chancellor, and of which he had had legal acquitment. This brought about the great scene at Northampton, where King and Archbishop met with their followers, like rival princes. Every insult was placed upon the Archbishop; his lodgings were occupied by the King's soldiers, who had to be ejected. When he confronted Henry, Henry refused to open his lips; and although he had come to meet him, forbade him the presence. Then on St. Edward's Day Thomas said Mass, put the Blessed Sacrament into a pyx, placed It on his breast, rode in full pontificals to the castle, took the Cross of Canterbury in his hand, and entered the outer presence chamber, beyond which he was forbidden to go. There he sat in awful silence. It was thought he would be murdered; almost all forsook him; Bishops threatened, entreated, wept. He sat immovable; soldiers made insulting gestures at him, while without the crowd of poor threatened any who laid a finger on him. At last the awful figure, by a mesmeric fascination, drew a crowd about it; then it rose, and Thomas spoke his mind. When the thunders were over, he swept from the hall, his Cross in hand, pursued with shrieks and curses and pelted with the rushes from the floor. The great door was locked; a big bunch of keys hung by it; a friend of the Archbishop seized the bunch, and the first key fitted. It was afterwards said that if the first key had not been the right one, the Archbishop would have been killed then. A massacre was expected in the monastery where the Archbishop was staying; they put his bed behind the High Altar for safety, and whispered Compline so as not to disturb him. It was a wild, wet night. Towards midnight four men mounted horses at the town gate, and rode to Grantham against the gale; and the next morning it was known at the Castle that the Archbishop had escaped.

For two years the Archbishop lived in the Cistercian Monastery at Pontigny. The King evicted all his dependents, and they came and lived round the Abbey. This made him sad, for he could do little for them. Otherwise he was happy. It was a two years' retreat; he sang in Choir, said Mass, worked in the fields, and was a simple Priest among the other Priests. During this time Europe paid attention to the quarrel, and it infuriated Henry by siding with Thomas. Henry had his barons and some Bishops; Thomas had the King of France, Pope Alexander III, the Churches of France and Italy, and the people of England. He remained absolutely immovable. At one time the Pope drew back from him, and then was sorry; at another

time the King of France did the same, and then
apologized on his knees. Thomas felt this was the
psychological moment, and he struck, and struck
hard. He had legatine powers, and he excom-
municated the Court Bishops, and threatened to
put Henry's Kingdom under an interdict.

It seems probable that it was then that Henry
decided to have him murdered. First he raised a
rebellion within the Church by getting the Archbishop of York to crown his son in the Province of
Canterbury. It is a technicality which it is not easy
for us to follow, but this act made the murder easier
by giving Henry more of the freedom of a private
person. And then he set himself to get Thomas
to return to England. He met him with all
courtesy; he bowed his head and begged his
blessing. He promised restitution on many
points. He did everything, except one thing. He
refused the Archbishop the official kiss of peace.
"My lord," said the King of France, "do not
return to England until you have received the kiss
of peace." And the Archbishop made a strange
reply, "God's Will be done." It was clear to anybody with Thomas' prophetic instinct that Henry
had fallen into the state of Saul in his latter days.
The Archbishop knew he was returning to his
death. He had fled as St. Cyprian fled, now he
returned as St. Cyprian returned, because he saw

that nothing but his death for his principles would change matters. His frightened followers suggested to him that he would probably be murdered when he landed, and he thought it well to give directions about the disposal of his body, but the people of England prevented that. He landed at Sandwich. As he was rowed ashore, the Cross of Canterbury borne aloft before him in the boat, he saw that the shore was black with people. They greeted him in a delirium of joy, shouting, " Blessed is he that cometh in the Name of the Lord." The Archbishop mounted, and with a great train rode to Canterbury; his path was challenged at one point by a body of angry soldiers, but they gave way before him, and he rode on. Canterbury held high festival—the streets were hung with tapestries and flowers, the bells rang out from every tower, the organs sounded in every church. Amid tumultuous shouts the Archbishop rode towards the Cathedral. Before he reached it he dismounted and went on, barefoot, to meet the monks who came out to greet him; then, leaving the shouts and flowers and music behind him, he entered the chapter house in solemn silence, and seating himself, preached a sermon to the ecclesiastics, and this was the text he chose, " We have here no continuing city; we seek one to come."

It was on the 1st of December that he landed;

there remained for him twenty-eight days more. He went to London, and was received with the same scenes—again the shouts and blessings and bells and flowers; but everywhere there was a feeling in the crowds that they were receiving the blessing of a martyr. He was to be at Canterbury for Christmas. "I go back," he said to the Abbot of St. Albans, "to celebrate such a Feast in my Church as Our Lord shall provide." He held his ordination in the cathedral on the Fourth Sunday in Advent. He sang the Midnight Mass, and the next morning preached, and also sang the High Mass of Christmas Day. On St. Stephen's Day he sent off several of his intimate friends on missions in different directions. That day and St. John's Day he sang Mass. On the Feast of the Innocents he heard Mass and passed the day quietly; at midnight he said Mattins with a few monks; afterwards he stood looking out into the darkness of the night, buried in thought.

Presently he said, "Could I, could I get to the coast before dawn?"

They said, "Yes, my lord, it is quite possible."

He stood silent; then he said in a low tone: "The Will of God must be done."

Hidden in Saltwood Castle at that moment there sat four men who also waited for the dawn, four men who had come to end this business of the

Archbishop : Fitzurse, de Tracy, de Morville, and le Breton, knights of the King.

On the morning of December 29th, 1170, the Archbishop of Canterbury heard Mass in his cathedral ; afterwards, he prayed before every Altar in the Church and received the discipline. Later on in the morning he made his confession. His Grace's dinner was served at three o'clock ; there were a few guests, among them his old schoolmaster, to whom he was devoted, and a clergyman from Cambridge named Edward Grim. The Archbishop made a good dinner, and talked delightfully all the time. Someone rallied him on his high spirits, and he smiled and said, " A man ought to be cheerful who is going to his Master."

Towards the end of dinner a servant said in a low voice, " My Lord, there are knights on their way here, sent by the King."

The Archbishop then said to the table, " I am about to die, but it will not happen here ; it will be inside the church."

He got up and went to his room, followed by his friends ; they sat down, and the Archbishop had just begun an ordinary conversation when the Seneschal came, white and trembling. " My Lord, the knights are here."

" Bid them come in." They entered, their

114

armour hidden under gowns, and sat down in front of the Archbishop.

He took no notice of them, and went on talking for a time. Then he turned, and after a long silence : " Well, Tracy," he said.

Fitzurse burst out, " God help you ! There is a message from the King. Shall it be public or private ? "

" As you please, as you please." The Archbishop signed to his friends to withdraw ; they waited trembling outside the door.

There were torrents of invective from the knights, broken sharply by the call of the Archbishop : " Come back and hear this. You can say to the King that the sea shall never again be between me and my Church, unless I am dragged hence by my feet."

He went on to argue patiently until Fitzurse shouted, " You accuse the King of falsehood."

" Reginald, Reginald," said the Archbishop, " I do no such thing ; you know these things are true."

At last the knights, who were strung up to a madness of anger, sprang to their feet and dashed their fists into the Archbishop's face.

The Archbishop rose : " Not all the swords in England drawn against me will force me from obedience to my God."

The knights, shouting "King's men! King's men!" rushed from the palace to fetch the soldiers they had brought. From all sides terrified servants rushed in, and the great doors of the palace were barred.

"My Lord, my Lord, they are arming without."

"What matter? Let them arm," rejoined the Archbishop, standing very grim and stiff.

In the distance, crashing blows on outer doors. "My Lord, my Lord, save yourself."

"Not I," said the Archbishop.

"My Lord, your presence is needed in the cathedral; vespers have begun."

This diplomacy was successful. "I will go to the cathedral," said the Archbishop; "bring my Cross, and carry it before me."

Canterbury Cathedral in the dark of a December afternoon, candle-light in the choir, and the rows of monks chanting vespers; but only the stalwarts are singing; the news has got in, and some are losing their heads. These ran down towards the cloister door; as they did so, the Cross of Canterbury entered, preceding His Grace the Archbishop.

"Come into choir, my Lord. Let us all die together."

"Get back to your place; I shall not come in till you are all back."

A tumult of people breaking in from the cloister.

Still the Psalms of Vespers, and now the beginnings of a great thunderstorm which was breaking over the city. Some of them try to bar the cloister door against the soldiers; but the Archbishop, using his great strength, hurls them right and left, and sets wide the door, saying in a voice of thunder, "I will not have my cathedral turned into a castle." A moment more and the murderers break in, followed by the soldiers. There is an attempt by his friends to drag the Archbishop into hiding; he flings them off, and they flee; three are left; one is the old schoolmaster, who sticks to his big boy right up to the end.

"Where is the traitor? Where is Thomas Becket?"

The great figure detached itself from the gloom, and came slowly down the choir steps to the transept. "Here I am, Reginald; no traitor, but a Priest of God."

They feared to murder him there, and tried to drag him from the church. "Do unto me here what you are going to do," said the Archbishop, and twined his great arms round a pillar. They could not move him, and drew back a little. Then the Archbishop knew the end had come; he stood forward, and, covering his face with his hands, prayed. Fitzurse feared a rescue. "Strike!" he screamed, "strike!" Tracy struck. Edward

Grim caught the blow on his arm, and the blow glanced off the head of the Archbishop. The Archbishop put up his hands, and, seeing the blood, cried; "Into Thy Hands, O Lord, I commend my spirit." A second blow. He remained standing still. A third, and he sank on his knees. On his knees, he turned to St. Benedict's altar, and joining his hands said in a low voice, "For the Name of Jesus, and in defence of the Church, I am willing to die." A fourth blow, and he fell forward on the pavement with his skull shattered. A fifth, and the brains of the martyr were scattered in sacrifice before the altar.

The lightning of God flared through the great windows, the thunderstorm crashed above the church, and the murderers fled into the darkness of the night.

So died St. Thomas of Canterbury, an Englishman in whom the spirit of St. Stephen lived again, who with St. Stephen stands in the Beatific Vision now. May his prayers aid us at the Throne of Grace to defend, even to the death—the Crib, the Cross, the Church, the Altar, and the Law of God!

THE LIFE AND DEATH OF
BLESSED THOMAS MORE

THREE hundred and fifty years have passed
and this is another England; we learn a
lesson from the fact. *At all times and in all places
the true servant of Jesus Christ is the same sort of
man.*

The Thames at Chelsea on a hot summer's day
in the early years of the sixteenth century, but such
a Thames and such a Chelsea as we have never seen,
for we are standing at a window in a beautiful Tudor
country house looking across lawns and gardens
to a sunlit river and a rural landscape beyond.

Below the river gate a barge is lying. We have
never seen such a magnificent barge nor such
gorgeous watermen as are lounging on the steps.

Three things have struck us about the beautiful house in which we are standing. Books and
musical instruments are scattered about; for the
master is a great student and an ardent musician.
There is a jolly sound of singing birds; his aviary
is celebrated. There are also several dogs and cats,
evidently on the best of terms with their surroundings.

All the people the house contains, from its mistress to its kitchen maids, are standing with their faces pressed to the windows. We are standing with the young people, grown-up Meg and her young husband, Cecily, John and their cousins and friends. In the centre oriel we observe a stout, reposeful-looking lady trying to conceal her curiosity behind a damask curtain. The gardens and lawns are empty. All eyes are turned towards a shrubbery on the right from which peals of laughter have burst from time to time. And then two figures come out of the shrubbery, one big, strong and burly, the other of medium height and slender. The arm of the big man is round the slighter man's neck and he keeps it there all the time as they slowly stroll towards the river, halting occasionally for the big man to have his laugh out. At the water's edge the guest gets into his barge and the host stands on the steps dismissing him with a courtesy which is indescribably charming because it is so careless, so unstudied, and so sweet. The strong oars of the watermen speed the boat off into the centre of the stream, and with a last, laughing, wave of the hand, the guest disappears from sight. The host, whose look has become a little wistful, turns back towards the house, from which a cataract of people tumbles out to greet him, the lady wife and the children, the cousins, the chaplain, the secretaries, the tutors, and all the servants, yes, even the page boys and the kitchen maids, for this is one great family bound together by every tie of love and religion, and they adore the figure who is strolling up the lawn.

"Oh, sir," says his son-in-law, Will Roper, "you are a happy man. There is no other man in the kingdom with whom the King would walk like that."

"He is indeed very kind to me, Will," replies Sir Thomas More, "but I have no cause to be proud of it, for if my head would win him a castle in this French war my head would not fail to go!"

Let us look at Thomas More as he stops to hug his children and caress his dogs on the lawn. His sensitive face is pale, with a flush in the cheeks, his hair is dark, his eyes are blue, a smile often flickers round his sensitive mouth. More was not expansive and rarely laughed. He was always happy and put everybody he met in a happy frame of mind. He was intensely fond of God's world and was interested and amused by everybody and everything. His wit and humour struck you first; he joked through life. One is soon bored by the chronic jester, but More never bored; he was the sweetest of fellows, with the soul of a Carthusian monk. Death was never far from his thoughts, and his Christlike love for this world made him long with ardent expectation for the next.

Thomas More's mother died when he was a baby, and he had no woman's love in his baby life. Happily his father sent him when a small boy to be page to Cardinal Morton at Lambeth Palace, and Thomas More became greatly devoted to the Cardinal, who was one of the best of men. He learnt to love Jesus and Mary at the Cardinal's feet. He was very studious and at thirteen talked Latin as well as he talked English. At fourteen he went up to the University of Oxford to learn Greek. Oxford was very stiff and monastic in those days. The learning of the Renaissance had reached it, but not its freedom and luxury. Sir John More did not give his son any pocket-money, and when he wanted his shoes mended Tom had to get the money from London. He did nothing but work hard for two years. Then his father brought him up to Lincoln's Inn and set him to study law. He was called to the Bar at twenty-three, and lectured in law for some years. At twenty-seven he was a member of Parliament.

When More came to London he took Dr. Colet, Dean of St. Paul's, the founder of the great St. Paul's school, now at Hammersmith, to be his confessor, and that brought him into the reforming

movement in the Church, and led to his friendship
with the great Erasmus.

He had taken a room near the Charterhouse
that he might attend the services in the Carthusian
chapel, and as time went on he began to wonder
whether he had a vocation for the religious life.
But his confessor said, " No, you have a vocation
for the married life."   So More married Jane Cole
and they had four children, and were as happy as
children themselves for five years.   Then Jane died,
and with her, youthful romance passed out of
More's life.   He needed a housewife and a guardian
for his orphaned babies, so he took Alice Middleton
for a second wife.   She was a strong, sensible,
reposeful woman, and his life remained a very
happy one, although Alice could not share his
deepest feelings, for she could not understand anything that seemed to pass the bounds of common-
sense.

We see More in his happiest moments when he
is with his children, and little cousin Maggie, whom
he had adopted, saying their prayers with them,
reading the Bible to them, and having tremendous
games with them.   He brought them presents
whenever he came home from his many journeys.
" For every stroke of the birch I give you," he said
once in a letter from France, " you know I give
you a hundred kisses."   The children laughed,

for father's birch was a bunch of peacock's feathers.

More loved all mankind and adored three people. The first in order of time was Erasmus, the great scholar of the age. These men, Colet, Erasmus and More were the modernists of those days, liberal Catholics. Would to God the Reformation, when it came, had been on their lines ! Colet and More were saints. Erasmus was not a saint, but he was a most fascinating person. More could see no imperfection in his " dear, darling Erasmus," while Erasmus used to say that he believed More to be the most witty man on earth, and that if More told him to dance on a tight-rope he should certainly try.

Then, as she grew to be his companion, Meg held the central place in his life, Meg, his eldest girl, who became Will Roper's wife. We shall see that before we end our tale.

More's third adoration was the King. For early in his life Henry VIII found he could not do without the company of the most brilliant, charming, lovable layman of the day, and he flung round More the spell of his fascination. As Brewer, the historian, writes, " To no other sovereign did his ministers ever dedicate themselves so utterly with head and heart, with body and soul. They craved for Henry's praise as hungry men crave for food."

Evening after evening the King and More sat talking about everything under the sun except politics, about art, poetry, divinity, geometry. Night after night they spent on the roof of the palace studying the stars. So often was More drawn into spending the evening with the King and Queen that he really set himself to be less attractive than he could be in order sometimes to get an evening at home at Chelsea.

Then at length Wolsey fell, and More was made Chancellor. He resigned himself to the post, but he foresaw it meant his final downfall and disgrace, because he knew he could not change the King, and that some day in conscience he would not be able to follow him. He was Lord Chancellor only three years, and resigned when he saw how things were going. He was prepared with great distaste to accept the divorce of Queen Katharine, and the Queenship of Anne Boleyn. It was a matter he felt in which the subject could not set himself against his sovereign, but when the King attached to the oath which pledged his subjects to acknowledge the succession through Queen Anne, a pledge to acknowledge himself Supreme Head of the Church in England, Thomas More's conscience forbade him to sign.

He held a very moderate view of the Papacy. Indeed he said once, " I was sometimes of a mind that there was nothing divine in its institution." That is not to be wondered at considering that the Pope during the years he was forming his opinions was Alexander VI. When the King wrote a strong passage in its defence in his book against Luther, More tried to get him to take the passage out or modify it. "I felt," he said, "that a question might well arise some day between the King and Pope." "I have never thought of the Pope as above an Œcumenical Council," he said, "and I have never greatly pressed the Pope's authority." "Indeed," he said, "I wrote a passage in favour of the Pope's authority which I cancelled when I saw that there was likely to be a feud between the Pope and the King." But his reading came to convince him of two points, first that the Primacy of the see of Peter is part of the Providence of God, the position of Lord Halifax to-day in his book on the Malines conversations. And, secondly, he became convinced that a secular prince cannot be head of the spirituality, the position of Bishop Hensley Henson's paper at the annual meeting of the English Church Union in 1930. When More decided that he could not take the oath, he did so not because he regarded the Papal primacy as a dogma all must hold, but because he himself held it to be true. He never tried to get anyone, not even his beloved Meg, to adhere to what he held to be a free opinion, but he said, "I hold it to be true and I must be true in conscience to my own point of view." He hoped that he might hold his opinion in silence, but that was not the Tudor way. He was required to speak.

So there came a day when he went down the lawn at Chelsea to take boat to Lambeth for what proved to be the last time. All the family came down to see him off as usual, but he stopped them on the lawn. "Don't come further to-day," he said, and going on without them he shut the door of the river archway behind him and embarked alone. Will Roper, his son-in-law, went with him. More was depressed and silent for a while, then he turned to Will with sunshine in his face. "I thank our Lord," he said, "the field is won."

At Lambeth the subscription to the oath went rapidly forward; nobles and bishops and priests queued up before the table at which the Archbishop, the Lord Chancellor, the Abbot of Westminster and the Lord Treasurer sat and signed right merrily. The Vicar of Croydon felt so jovial that he asked for a drink, and was shown the way to the buttery.

More was shown into a little room to think matters over. While he was there Dr. Hugh Latimer and some chaplains and secretaries went into the garden shouting with laughter. Latimer, with his arms round the necks of two of the

127

chaplains, pulled them hither and thither in a wild romp.

And now he was before the Archbishop. " I notice, Sir Thomas," said the Archbishop, " that you do not condemn those who subscribe but that you are not sure you can do so yourself. You regard the matter therefore as uncertain. On the other hand you are certain of your duty to the King. One ventures to think that if you refuse to sign you are as good as subscribing to a thing you regard as uncertain, while if you sign you are subscribing to what you regard as certain." It was perhaps not the only time in history when this kindly voice has been heard at Lambeth.

" I attach great weight," replied Sir Thomas, " to anything your Grace may say, but I feel this a matter in which I cannot take that line."

" May I venture, Sir Thomas," said the Abbot of Westminster, " very humbly to suggest, that it may be a little—may I say?—presumptuous to oppose one's opinion to that of the great council of the realm ? "

" But, Father Abbot, I fancy I should have a General Council of the Church behind me."

" More," said the Lord Treasurer, " I would rather my own boy lost his head than that you should take this line. What will the King say, man ? What will he do ? "

"Well," said the prisoner, "whatever the result, I cannot prevent it without peril to my soul."

But the commissioners were sincerely moved. "Look here," said Cranmer, "we must get the oath changed. The King must drop the preamble about the authority. Then the Bishop of Rochester and More will sign."

"I will go to the King," said the Treasurer.

But the King was in a black rage and immovable. So they brought Sir Thomas to the Tower of London. The porter asked for his perquisite— the prisoner's hat.

"Dear me," said the prisoner, "I am sorry, I am afraid it is very shabby."

More was exceedingly happy in the Tower. He had always longed for more time for prayer, and he lived as much as possible like a religious solitary. He suffered physically a good deal, for he had that most painful ailment, stone. He had had chronic bronchitis for some time, and at night had terrible cramps in the legs, but on his better days, Meg, who was allowed to visit him often, in the hope of shaking him, found him very cheery. They would say their psalms and a litany together, and then have a jolly time.

Towards the end of the year Parliament passed an Act proclaiming the King head of the Church of England. They now isolated More. Meg

might not come again. They took away his
writing things, but using stray scraps of paper and
writing with a piece of coal or a charred stick, he
still got messages home to Chelsea. These were
messages of tender farewell, and now he spent part
of every night in prayer. Months passed, and on
May 6th Meg came for the last time. She had put
before him the reasonableness of his doing what
so many good men had done, and what he had
never advised her not to do, but she knew he was
immovable and had ceased to press it. The last
day she was allowed to come was the day of the
martyrdoms of the Carthusians, and leaning on
Meg's shoulder More watched them go to death
from the window of his cell. On the 9th he
received a visit from the Archbishop, the Lord
Chancellor, the Duke of Norfolk, and Lord
Wiltshire. "The King commands us to tell you
that your silence is inadmissible. He demands
your opinion of the new statute."

"I must remain silent," said More. "I am not
worthy to offer myself for death. I might fall
through presumption."

They left him for some weeks. On July 1st he
was brought out of prison, now an old, bent man
with a grey beard, and tried for high treason in
Westminster Hall. "Is the new statute, prisoner,
right or wrong?"

"I decline to say, my lords, and I remind you that you cannot condemn a man for silence."

"You are adjudged," said the lords, "guilty of high treason."

"Since I am condemned," said the prisoner, "I will now speak plainly. A temporal lord ought not, cannot be, head of the spirituality."

As he went down to the boat the people looked with awe, and somewhere near the tube station where the motor traffic roars to-day, John More, his son, knelt in silence before him to receive his blessing. The people felt as though the Host were passing.

Silently the boat went down the stream, and presently More saw that the constable of the Tower, sitting by his side, was weeping. "My dear good Kingston," he said, "do not grieve. You and your wife and I will be very merry in heaven."

On the Tower wharf he was surrounded by guards through whom a figure broke, and once more Meg was in his arms. They let him hold her there for some time to comfort her, and when, as they reached the gate, she broke through once more, they stood silent around, the tears falling down their cheeks, until the soldiers drew her gently away. The night before he died her father sent her one more message. "Your love," he said, "never helped me more than on the wharf when we parted. It will be, I hope, to-morrow morning; to-morrow is the Eve of St. Thomas of Canterbury and the Octave of SS. Peter and Paul, so I long to go to God to-morrow. Farewell, dear child, and pray for me as I shall for you and all your friends, that we may meet merrily in heaven."

At daybreak the next morning his very old friend, Sir Thomas Pope, was allowed to come and tell him that it was to be before nine o'clock. When they parted the martyr was smiling and his friend was in tears. When he was alone More dressed himself for a great festival. He put on his very best clothes and a magnificent gown of damask and fur.

At a quarter to nine the lieutenant of the Tower entered his cell to conduct him to the scaffold. "My dear friend," he said, "please do not wear that gown; it will become the property of a low fellow, and we should be terribly shocked to see him wearing it."

"But," said More, "he is going to do me such a favour that I might fitly give him cloth of gold."

The lieutenant remained so distressed that More said, "Well, well, to please you I will change it," and he put on a gown of frieze. "But I have so little money left," he said. "However, I have one gold angel and I will give him that."

As they crossed Tower Hill a good woman

offered him a cup of wine. He thanked her smilingly, but he would not take it. Our Lord, he remembered, had refused an anodyne. "Come, lieutenant," he said when they reached the scaffold, "this platform is a bit shaky. Help me up, and I will look after myself coming down."

He looked round on the scaffold and said, "I hope you will all pray for me. I die for the Faith of the Holy Catholic Church, a faithful servant of God and the King." Then he knelt down and with deep devotion said the *Miserere*.

"I ask your pardon, sir," said the executioner, "for what I am going to do."

More put his arms round him. "You could not do me a greater kindness," he said; "cheer up, dear fellow, don't be afraid to do your duty, my neck is very short, so be careful to keep up your reputation. I will cover my eyes myself; I have brought a handkerchief for the purpose."

He laid his head on the block. "Stop a moment, let me put my beard out of the way. That never committed high treason. Now."

And so the fatal blow was struck, and he heard the great "Well done." "For," said Addison, writing two hundred years after, "he did not look on the severing of his head from his body as a circumstance that ought to produce any change in the disposition of his mind."

ST. FRANCIS DE SALES

HIS Holiness the Pope has pointed out that Francis de Sales was given to the Church for a particular purpose, to demonstrate that true sanctity is possible for persons immersed in the ordinary affairs of the life of the modern world, and in giving the Saint to be the Patron of Journalists and other writers who defend the Christian religion or base their work on its philosophy, His Holiness bids them imitate the vigour and firmness, the moderation and charity of the Saint.

At first sight, perhaps, it might be thought that the literary world would not be quite at its ease with St. Francis. We associate some measure of unconventionality with literary persons, and at first sight Francis seems oppressingly conventual. He really lived like a skylark in a heavy gilded cage, but it was part of his saintliness to be quite happy inside the bars.

He was an awfully—I use the word in its true sense—an awfully good little boy. It gratifies our frailty to learn that he once stole from a workman employed at his father's château a gay shoulder-knot—I suppose its equivalent to-day would be a flashing tie-pin—but our spirits sink again when we find that he confessed his sin immediately on being questioned and took the tremendous public thrashing his father gave him like a little angel.

Francis, you remember, was practically the contemporary of Shakespeare. His aristocratic and wealthy father and mother, M. and Madame de Boisy—the Count de Sales had taken his wife's name—were among the great personages of Savoy. They were ardent Catholics, living in all the strictness of the first days of the Counter-Reformation, with Calvinism entrenched as a strong armed state next door. They thought of the Calvinists as English Conservatives think of Bolsheviks. De Boisy was a great character, a splendid, lovable fellow, boisterous and tyrannical, but truly warmhearted and religious. Though he had a good deal of the Three Musketeers about him, he was a character for Molière rather than for Dumas ; he was a typical Tory diehard Squire, with Catholic, instead of Protestant, prejudices. " There is only one way of converting these fellows—the cannon's mouth," he roared, when his wonderful saintly son set off to preach the Catholic Gospel again in the Chablais, where the people had been made Protestants by the method M. de Boisy was recommending to Catholics. We seem to recall our foxhunting uncle discussing the Sinn Feiners over his port.

The conventions of the grandparents of the people whom Velasquez painted must have been terribly ponderous, and it is a miracle that Francis, the eldest son, who was bear-led by a ferocious clerical tutor, grew up as he did. He accepted the conditions of his life with perfect content; that was part of his mission; but although he was astoundingly good you would have all fallen in love with him, full of sweetness and charm, a perfect dancer, a splendid rider, a brilliant swordsman and a keen student. His intolerable success at Padua led to his being waylaid and attacked at night by a group of enemies. It was a scene from *The Three Musketeers*; Francis and his sword playing d'Artagnan against the gang; Francis flying after the frightened ringleader, sword in hand, and inflicting sharp punishment. There was another scene more dramatic still. The party of disorder in the University of Padua introduced a woman of light character to Francis in the guise of a lady in distress who needed chivalrous help. Francis, who was an exceedingly wide-awake young man with the instincts of a great gentleman, read the lady's character at once and dealt with the situation summarily.

Just at about this time he had a terrible illness

and was at the point of death. He made his dispositions with care, for he was always a great man of business, and bequeathed his body to be dissected by the students at the Padua School of Anatomy.

"What a horrible suggestion!" said his grief-stricken tutor.

"I have never done any good, living," said the moribund Francis, "and I should like to be a bit of use when I am dead."

He did not die. He decided to be ordained and had a tremendous battle over it with his father. M. de Boisy, who had a career and a wife arranged for his eldest son, refused to see him made a priest. He was only partly reconciled when family influence got the young man made Provost of the Cathedral Chapter and the leading Priest of his Diocese while he was still a lay youth in his father's house. It was as though a Duke of Marlborough might be induced to allow a Marquis of Blandford to be ordained if Mr. Winston Churchill could get him made Dean of Christ Church while still a layman of twenty-one.

Observe Francis' attitude; he accepted this as a God-sent plan for enabling him to be ordained, and in seven months he was a Priest. He accepted the exceedingly unideal ecclesiastical situation, and by adorning it as a Saint immeasurably improved it. These people had seen the evils of Reformation by revolt; they were all set upon Reformation through permeation, a much more difficult matter. Ignatius Loyola had led the way, Vincent de Paul was to carry on the task. Both these men were priests, Ignatius with a great deal of liberty, Vincent with a certain amount. Francis' path was the hardest of all, the path of the Reformer in high ecclesiastical office. The Provost did not do his work from his decanal stall. He offered to go as a missionary into the Chablais, a sub-Alpine region which had been captured for Protestantism by force of arms. M. de Boisy felt he had been deceived, as a Duke of Marlborough would if his Dean of Christchurch established himself in Moscow with the forlorn hope of converting a Bolshevik or two and the certainty of being killed by the Union of Soviet Republics.

Francis loved his father devotedly, and it was one of the sharpest pangs of his life to go to his dangerous work without his father's blessing. But the old man was the best of good fellows and he came to see the point. He came to see that this was a military mission of a very honourable sort, in which the Cross, not the sword, was the weapon. Few stories tell more clearly the supernatural character of Catholicism than the story of Francis and his family. He withstood them like a rock when they opposed his vocation, but he became the Confessor of his father, mother and brothers and the light and guide of their lives.

No missionary has ever endured a greater variety and subtlety of suffering than Francis, the Provost, did in his mission to the Chablais. They entitle him to be Patron Saint of all war correspondents. He had to say Mass a long distance from his lodging. He used to stain the frozen roads with blood from his terrible chilblains day after day. He had to cross a roaring torrent on his path by crawling over a frozen board on hands and knees. He once saved himself from being frozen to death by hiding for the night in the village oven, still warm from the last baking. He once spent a night up in a tree fastened to a bough by his cincture, to escape from the wolves who gathered underneath. Next morning he was too hard frozen to move, and people had to lower him to the ground with cords. This was one of the turning-points, for those who lowered him began to listen to him. His life was, of course, often attempted, but nobody succeeded in killing him.

But far worse than this was the atmosphere of hatred in which he lived, the sense of which never left him. His goodness and power at first seemed useless ; they were ascribed to Satan ; but conscious

of the authority behind him he never wavered.
He was a great propagandist, one of the first to
recognize the power of the press, and where people
refused to hear him preach he papered the place
with tracts. Sensitive souls shrink from controversy and are applauded for doing so; it is a
shining jewel in Francis' crown that he did not.
He showed the modern world a saint contending
for the faith. This work went on for ten years.
When the State found he was becoming successful
it backed him up. He approved of this backing,
and indeed demanded it. In dealing with heresy,
as in all else, it was his mission to be part of his
age, not a critic of his age. He was meant to be
the leaven leavening the lump, not the pioneer
flashing on and leaving his contemporaries behind.

After the excitements of the Chablais there
remain twenty years during which his life seems
set in a heavy, uninteresting frame. Bad health
and dull, wearisome, monotonous business must
have been his greatest trials, yet he never seems
to have been tempted to the sin of *accidie*. He
was, first, coadjutor to the Bishop of Geneva and
then Bishop Granier's successor, with his Seat at
Annecy, because the Calvinists held Geneva. We
see Francis mostly in his scattered mountainous
diocese, its unwearied pastor, going about it very
much as Bishop King went about Lincolnshire,

cheering lonely *curés* and blessing lonely shepherds. But he was often at the Court of Savoy, sometimes at the Court of Rome, sometimes with Henry IV in Paris. He won an immense reputation as a preacher and director. We see, what in our world is an unknown sight, a brilliant dissolute society applauding that shining flower of humanity, adoring and surrounding Catholic Saintliness as soon as it recognizes it. Henry IV of France, who resembled our Edward VII in many ways, was devoted to Francis. "He is a man of good blood," he said, "with every virtue, and no faults; he is gentle, affable and humble, always in complete control of himself; he is full of piety, with no affectation and no scrupulosity."

"M. de Genève," said the King one day, "I wish you would stay here by me. I can give you a much better position than any in Savoy."

"No, Sire," said Francis laughing, "I have married a poor wife and I must not leave her for a richer one."

It was a weary, weary life; it tires one to think of it. Francis of Assisi threw his purse into the bushes for God's sake. For God's sake Francis de Sales kept accounts and was faithful to the death in all those irksome tasks pertaining to a complicated life which Francis of Assisi shed the day he stepped out of his clothes in his father's presence and walked away naked into the world. He shows us endless perseverance in doing dull things. He exhibits the grace which comes from serving tables, when serving tables means a lowly way of doing the highest work. He heard multitudes of confessions, he directed many people, he was never too busy to help tiresome people. He sat up all night writing letters. Journalists should remember this; their Patron Saint is the Saint of the midnight oil. His pastoral love and zeal filled all this tiresome life with joy, for Francis, often sick and always driven, was a very happy man. He had three especial loves—poor people, the world of nature, and the world of children.

He kept up the state of a Catholic Bishop in a very modest way, for, like his Patron of Assisi, his heart was always with the poor. His books show us his love of nature, which spoke to him in lovely parables all day long. And of course all the children adored him.

"What a draught," he said one day in a convent parlour and got up to shut the door and then sat down again leaving it open.

"But, Monseigneur, you have not shut the door," said the Lady Abbess.

"I can't," whispered the Bishop with a laughing face, "the children are outside; they are all watching me."

142

We all know the Devout Life and the Letters; they are delightfully cheerful, tender, sensible and funny. Francis always suggests that it is sheer common sense and also great fun to try to be good. The two elements in the life of piety are self-discipline and love. Francis looks chiefly to love, and he is always insisting that self-discipline must be practised from the motive of love. "Live," he says, "a life of loving, simple, generous fidelity to the will of God. Keep our Lord always before your eyes, study His Features and do your actions as He did His." Francis' main purpose in life was to give this message as clearly as possible; with this object he formed his literary style, aiming at the greatest simplicity, directness and clearness, and in so doing he formed the modern French language. This is a point on which I can only re-peat what we are told—that the limpidity, delicacy, sensitiveness of the best modern French had its origin in the style of St. Francis de Sales. It is this which gives Francis the right to be the Patron Saint of Christian letters. By forming his style for the noblest reason, to speak as plainly as he could of God to man, he unfolds the highest mission of language and literature.

"You are pastors and teachers," he says to writers. "Write so as to give your message in the purest, simplest form." And in this he would be echoed by two of the greatest masters of Modern English—by Newman and by Church. But his deepest message to literary men is found in his profound reverence for all life. He saw the best that was to be seen in all men and all things; he saw it, he loved it, he appealed to it and so made it still better.

" Look," he says to them, " with profound reverence upon all life in this world. Try to see in true perspective all ranks of society, try to value at their true worth all the institutions of Church and realms. You have a great responsibility in this matter because you have dedicated your lives to the task of analysing, recording and commenting upon the human scene. You observers of the life of your time stand at the sources of history. You are the makers, then, of the raw material which future ages will take up and weave into the history of the human race."

Such, I conceive, to be his charge to men of letters, and a study of his writings will help them to obey him. Francis, who had lived the hardest of lives in the seats of the mighty, died with delightful ease and naturalness. In 1622 he had been bidden to accompany the Court of the Duke of Savoy into France on a visit of ceremony to King Louis XIII. As usual he obeyed, though far from well. On the return journey he put up in Lyons at the gardener's cottage of one of the Convents of the Visitation which he and St. Jean Francis de Chantal had founded. On the Feast of St. John the Evangelist he had a grave seizure in the poor little cottage bedroom, made his profession of Faith, and with great tranquillity received the last Sacraments.

From that moment he turned his face to God like a tired child. He never spoke his beautiful French again, but only a few Bible words in Latin. " I have waited for the Lord," he was heard to murmur, " and He inclined unto me and heard my complaint."

Later on a friend recalled him with a gentle pressure of the hand, and Francis smilingly whispered, " It is towards evening and the day is far spent." Afterwards he lay in great quietude. Just before the end the listener caught one more gentle sound ; it was the Holy Name of Jesus.

The Feast of the Holy Innocents was dawning, and it was the Holy Innocents and not any greater personages that those about him invoked to his aid ; and so when the last silence fell I think of Francis as being pulled by a flock of cheering, laughing babies into the presence of our Lord.

" IF Keble is my fire," said Hurrell Froude to Newman, " I am Keble's poker," and the story of Hurrell Froude is the story of how the poker poked the fire at which Newman came to warm himself and bring fresh fuel to the flames.

This fire which had always burned in Keble before Hurrell and Newman made it blaze was not of Keble's kindling. It was the Holy Fire of Catholic faith and practice handed on through the centuries and conserved from childhood in Keble's heart and soul, for his father had handed on to his boy the cavalier and non-juring tradition. Indeed to those who are disposed to say that continuity in the English Church can only have consisted in a mechanical transmission of Apostolic Orders, the heart and soul of John Keble are a sufficient and a living answer, for Keble always said that the Oxford Movement only expanded what his father had taught him.

John Keble was the son of a country parson who would not let his boy go to a boarding school, who prepared him for Oxford himself and sent him up to Corpus with a classical scholarship at the age of fourteen. He came up a fresh, glad, bright, joyous boy, and found himself living in a small society of men, fifty all told. The fifty men (this is a pleasant story) took the boy to their hearts, and in this kindly warmth all the happy fun of his home life reappeared at college and is reflected in his letters to his people.

In 1810, when he was eighteen, the boy took a double first in classics and mathematics, to which he afterwards added the Chancellor's Prizes for Latin and English Essays. Still with the manners of a shy, sensitive, retiring freshman, he was hailed as the most brilliant graduate of the time. In 1811, when he was 19, he was elected to a fellowship at Oriel.

Copleston's Oriel was not unlike Jowett's Balliol. "We are fellows of Oriel College. What we know not is not knowledge," was the unspoken slogan of the common room. After the home life in Corpus, Keble was never able to like the tone of the Oriel common room, which seemed to him rough and irreverent. By nature he was a poet, through grace a pastor of souls and lover of the poor. He was ordained on his fellowship, Deacon in 1815, Priest in 1816. But his fellowship did not at that time carry a tutorship, he had nothing to do, and his sister Sarah's death drew him back to his father's house (the strength of family affection played a large part in the lives of the Oxford

Leaders). Keble worked as curate of two little neighbouring parishes for two happy years, and was then called back to Oriel to take up a tutorship. The return to college life meant exchanging the spiritual care of some few hundred Gloucestershire peasants for the academical care of a dozen young gentlemen. But in each of these boys this strange new tutor saw a soul to be led into communion with God. " The salvation of one soul," he said, " is worth more than the framing of the Magna Carta of a thousand worlds." He did not preach to them, but he got up at six o'clock in the morning to help his pupils with their work.

Keble lived this life for six years, but all the while he was longing for his simple life among the poor, and when his mother died in 1823 his love for his family sent him back once more to the neighbourhood of Fairford to be a solace to his father. He returned to the peasants he had taught before, and became curate of Southrop, where there was a good-sized house in which he felt he could keep his hold on some of his Oxford pupils who might come to him as his guests. Three boys followed him to spend their long vacations at Southrop—Robert Wilberforce, the brother of the bishop, Isaac Williams, son of a Cardiganshire gentleman who had come up from Harrow to Trinity, and Richard Hurrell Froude.

Hurrell Froude was the son of the Archdeacon of Totnes, and his home was his father's rectory on the banks of the Dart. He had been brought up to be an established member of the Established Church of the reign of George IV. His father, the archdeacon, did his duty admirably in the state of life into which it had pleased God to call him. He was an excellent artist in water colours, highly educated, and, as Keble once said, provokingly intelligent, so much so that he was quite uncomfortable to think of, making one ashamed, Keble added, of going gawking about the world without understanding anything one sees. Archdeacon Froude was a good specimen of the superior clergy of his day, with whom, as a result of the French Revolution, the squirearchy had made an alliance, and who were, generally speaking, benevolent to their parishioners, useful to the county, justices of the peace, men who shot and hunted moderately, and dined occasionally with the Lord Lieutenant.

Hurrell had a deep respect for his father, but all the emotional side of his nature he had drawn from his beautiful, sympathetic and imaginative mother, who had died when Hurrell was a little boy, and sorrow and longing for his mother were always the underlying notes of his loving, sensitive, impetuous, headstrong young life.

There is a picture of Hurrell when he was fourteen, a fine head, dark hair falling over a noble forehead, a long oval face, a straight nose, a well-shaped, determined mouth and chin, large dark eyes set rather far apart, which look out of the picture wistfully, inquiringly, sadly. " I should like to talk to that boy," you feel.

When he was almost a baby his father sent Hurrell to school at Ottery St. Mary, where his house-master was the brother of the poet Coleridge. At thirteen the boy went to Eton. He went up to Oriel as a Commoner in 1821, when he was eighteen, and for the next two years was one of Keble's pupils. At this time Hurrell was a very handsome youth, tall, erect and slim, with a face which showed every mood of playfulness, sadness and awe. He never spared himself. Newman said that there was a fiery force in his look and tone which made him seem a sort of angelic presence to weaker natures. They say his friends would provoke him to attack them in order to be disarmed at last by his enchanting smile. Hurrell loved doing what it is difficult and dangerous to do. Like his father, the archdeacon, he was a daring cross-country rider. Living on the lovely and lotus-eating banks of the Dart, Hurrell was for the open sea ; he loved to sail his own boat through rough weather, and was a skilled seaman.

He flung himself into all the outdoor games and
exercises of Oxford life, sailing, skating, riding—
it was before the days of torpids and eights—and
continued when he became a tutor to head his
pupils in the field, the olive-crowned Youth of the
Olympic games. Hurrell was also a very keen
mathematician, absorbed in the practical details of
mechanics and hydrostatics. Newman said he had
no particular taste for theology, but it was a time
when people were bringing to England the fruits
of the Grand Tour, and Hurrell conceived a passion
for the Gothic architecture of the continent, which
sent his spirit of adventure off in an ecclesiastical
direction. He had a love for all things bright
and beautiful in nature and in art, and would have
been supremely happy in the household of Sir
Thomas More.

When Keble took Hurrell to stay with him at
Southrop, he also took, as I have said, Robert
Wilberforce, very much absorbed in his work for
the schools, and Isaac Williams, of Trinity, whom
Keble's pastoral instinct had recognized to be in
more urgent need of spiritual help than the other
two.

Isaac Williams, sensitive and poetical, had been
sent to a bad preparatory school, and had gravi-
tated into an unsatisfactory set at Harrow. He
won the Latin Verse Prize in 1823, and this brought

him into contact with Keble, who, I think, was one of the adjudicators.

Finding that Isaac ought to be reading, and had made no plans for the vacation, Keble said, " I am now leaving Oxford for good, suppose you come and read with me ? "

" If a merciful God had miraculously interposed to arrest my course," says Isaac Williams, " I could not have had a stronger assurance of His Presence than I have always had in looking back on that day."

To these three boys Keble was a revelation. They were all brilliant, keen scholars, and here was the most distinguished figure of their Oxford leaving the university at the height of his fame, with every prospect open to him, to devote himself to Gloucestershire peasants, and treating them with the deepest love and respect, and with no sense whatever of having made a sacrifice. " I could not understand," said Isaac Williams, " such love in thought and action as he showed me ; he opened a new world to me."

Keble had never been so happy and gay, ready at all times for any sort of exercise, mental or physical. " There's Master," said his gardener, " the greatest boy of them all."

But it was to Hurrell Froude that Keble mattered most.

Keble filled the place in young Hurrell's heart that the death of his mother had left empty. The boy was like a high-bred unmanageable horse responding at once to the magic touch of a horse-trainer. Keble's goodness and purity humbled Hurrell secretly to the dust and disposed him to accept without reserve his master's teaching. On the other hand the older man gave to the younger all the tenderness of the spiritual father. Gradually Keble got to know something of the exquisite sensitiveness, the agonizing conscientiousness, the tearful penitence and devoutness of the inner life which Hurrell's journal reveals.

In the private intercourse of these two the Oxford Movement came to the birth. Hurrell took Keble's religion to be his own, and under his merciless cross-questioning, Keble's ecclesiastical principles became more clear cut. Somebody, Mozley or Isaac Williams, says, " Hurrell Froude catechized Keble into definiteness."

What emerged was as follows. Keble could not be satisfied with the Church of the eighteenth century with which Dr. Johnson had been fairly satisfied, and he felt that the evangelicalism of one hundred years ago, the current revulsion from the eighteenth century, was trusting too much to emotion and too little to disciplined character. So he fell back, and here is the beginning of the

Movement, on the conception of the Church he had inherited, a body independent of the State, founded by our Lord Himself, in direct succession from the Apostles, one in continuous history and devotion with the Apostolic Church, filled with a supernatural and sacramental life, witnessing to a lofty moral standard before the world.

Possessed by this vision, Hurrell began by trying to discipline his own private life on Catholic lines, and the private journal is the story of the determined efforts of the splendid headstrong boy to break his will, destroy his pride, and curb his passions. It is the revelation of the making of a saint.

But there was a certain excessiveness about Froude which appears in his efforts, and in his arguments. He seems to be fighting himself for Christ when he should have been yielding himself to Christ, and in the vehemence of his controversy he would antagonize people or frighten them. He never frightened or antagonized Keble, but he sometimes made Keble anxious. Hurrell used to defend his startling way of saying things on the ground that it was the only way of getting people's attention. " When you had done that," he used to say, " you might modify your statements." Remember he was dealing with the world of Jane Austen's novels, and to break up the polished

surface of the society of that day you needed somebody with a merciless logical force like the drill
which breaks up the surface of a London street.
This was Hurrell's contribution to the Movement;
the instrument which poked up Keble's fire was
also capable of smashing up the conventions and
proprieties of Edmund Bertram of *Mansfield Park.*

Changes in Keble's life dissolved the Southrop
group after two years, and for the rest of their
lives the friendship with Hurrell Froude was kept
up largely by correspondence. Hurrell took his
degree in 1824, getting seconds in Greats and
Mathematics. He was elected a fellow of Oriel
in 1826, and became a tutor in 1827, being ordained
deacon in 1828, and priest in 1829.

When Froude became a tutor Newman had been
one for a year, and now began a friendship based
upon the common aims of the two men in their
tutorial work, the aims of shepherds of souls. For
Hurrell had the aim to be to his pupils what Keble
was to him, and he found in Newman a glorious
ally.

Newman was the son of a London banker and
a French Huguenot mother. He was a born
musician who wrote an opera when he was ten,
and would have been a Kreisler if he had given
himself to the violin. Soon after he went up to
Trinity College, Oxford, Newman's father lost all

his money, and his thoughts, like Manning's years afterwards, were thus forcibly turned away from a worldly career. In 1823, the year Keble carried off Hurrell to Southrop, Newman was elected a Fellow of Oriel, and until 1825 he worked under Dr. Whateley, who afterwards became Archbishop of Dublin, as vice-principal of St. Alban Hall. Whateley was a Liberal, a broad churchman who had shed his Erastianism with his conservatism, and had developed a theory of the Church which was largely the Catholic one and attracted Newman's attention. Under Whateley's influence Newman passed from his early Calvinism through a Liberal and questioning period of thought, carrying on with him and developing Whateley's theory of the Church. He had the loftiest conception of the pastoral office, and the tutorship which he undertook at Oriel in 1826 drew out his love of souls. Gradually, from his sympathy with the pastoral beauty of Keble's character as it began to be interpreted to him by Hurrell Froude, Newman began to love Keble from afar and absorb his principles. Keble, it will be remembered, had ceased to live in Oriel the year Newman arrived there, and Newman tells us that it was the question of the nature of a tutor's office which drew him and Froude and Keble into personal co-operation.

Newman was horrified at the coarse drinking

ways of the men, and at the tutors' attitude of having no responsibility for conduct which did not actually break college rules. At once he began to shepherd his men, and evoked in them that hero worship which is so easy to young men. It is always fascinating to be tenderly shepherded by a genius.

In 1826 Robert Wilberforce and Hurrell Froude became tutors, and Newman found that, inspired by Keble, they felt the same responsibility for the souls of their pupils as he did. And now came the incident which determined the course of events. Dr. Copleston was made Bishop of Llandaff, and the Provostship fell vacant. There was one obvious man in residence, Edward Hawkins, the best specimen of the existing *régime*. Against him the Fellows who were his disciples voted for the saintly absent Keble, who had never been very happy in the Oriel common room. Newman who hardly knew Keble, and Pusey who had been elected Fellow the year Keble went out of residence, voted for Hawkins. Hurrell Froude had fought for Keble, saying he would bring in a new world, but Newman laughed and said, "If it were an Angel's place I should vote for Keble, but we are only electing a Provost."

Hawkins was elected, and in his sermon at the consecration of Keble chapel, Pusey lamented the mistake they had made. But Newman thought otherwise; he felt that if it had been possible to make Oriel an ideal Christian college under Keble, they might all have been content with that, and might have settled down in Oriel and lived happy ever after.

As it was the new Provost disapproved of the pastoral influence he and Hurrell were exercising over their pupils. He thought that the pastoral and academic offices could not and should not be combined. He felt that Newman and Froude were making an inner circle in the college which was breaking up its unity. This gave to Newman and Froude a wider view of the situation. The trouble lay in the fact that a high-minded man like the Provost was not moved to any action by the unworthy character of the social life of the younger men. The whole English outlook had to be altered. Keble was teaching that the Church existed to do what was wanted, and could do it when inspired to live again the life God had ordered. They realized that their reformed Oriel would be a new patch on an old garment, further that they could not reform Oriel until they had reformed England. So the prophets, finding themselves without honour in their own country, turned their thoughts towards the Church and world of the English people.

The Provost announced (it was all done in a friendly way) that after a certain time he did not propose to assign to these tutors any more pupils. Froude resigned his tutorship, Newman worked on with his diminishing band until the last of them had taken his degree. This happened in the summer of 1831, and, early in the long vacation, feeling free of care for the moment, Newman went down for the first time to Dartington to stay with Hurrell Froude.

It was the year before the Reform Bill, and the violent, threatening temper of the English people seemed heading towards a French Revolution. No one knew how events would turn ; everything English was in the melting-pot. It was clear that all except the high Tories would turn against the Church of England. Bereft of their pupils, and set free to think, both men saw that high Toryism, of which Froude had always been the somewhat truculent champion, had no principle through which it could save the Church, that the Church could only be saved by revealing her true character to men, and inspiring her to display it once more fully to the world.

The Movement was beginning, but without as yet recognizing itself. It had begun in Keble's life and teaching, in the awful sincerity of the self-discipline of Hurrell's inner life, and in the same sincerity of those parochial sermons at St. Mary's, Oxford, where Newman, now its vicar, was rebuking by contrast the loose unreality of the churchmanship of the day.

The friends went by boat from Southampton to Torquay, travelling by night. Newman refused to sleep in the hot and crowded cabin, and they spent the night on deck wrapt in cloaks and blankets, and rocked by the heavy swell they encountered off Portland Bill. That night Hurrell caught a heavy cold. It was the beginning of the first great influenza epidemic, and when they got to Dartington they found the whole household prostrate. Newman expected to catch it and did not, but influenza seized Hurrell Froude on top of his heavy cold and this was the beginning of the illness from which five years afterwards he died.

Wandering about alone during the illness of his hosts Newman registered a vow. He had never been in South Devon before, and its softness, richness and colour, the extreme deliciousness of its air and the fragrance of everything, appealed to all the sensuous side of his nature. He describes his feelings in a letter to his sister. " Really, I think," he says, " that I should dissolve into essence of roses or be attenuated into an echo if I lived here; the exuberance of the grass and foliage is oppressive, as if one had not room to breathe;

160

the depths of the valleys, the steepness of the
slopes increase the illusion. The scents are very
fine and the colours of the flowers as though they
were shot with white. The sweet peas especially
have the complexion of a beautiful face. They
trail up the walls mixed with myrtles as creepers.
As to the sunsets, the Dartmoor heights look
purple, and the sky close upon them a clear orange.
I think of Virgil's description of the purple meads
of Elysium."

Hurrell Froude used to say that Hamlet should
be bound up with the Georgics of Virgil. But
it was himself wandering through the groves of
Dart that Hurrell saw in that strange volume. For
a feeling was growing among the men of the Movement that they had a work to do, and must beware
of being captured by nature or by art.

And at Dartington Newman made a vow and
registered it in verse :

There strayed awhile amid the woods of Dart
  One who could love them but who durst not love.
A vow had bound him, ne'er to give his heart
  To streamlet bright, or soft secluded grove.
'Twas a hard humbling task onwards to move
His easy captured eye from each fair spot,
  With unattached and lonely step to rove
O'er happy meads which soon its print forgot,
Yet kept he safe his pledge, prizing his pilgrim lot.

Newman went back to Oxford. The influenza

which had swept England died away. Various plans for future work were made and dropped. Hurrell remained ill at home, and early in 1832 wrote a bad report of the condition of his throat to Newman. His father became anxious and told Newman that he was advised that Hurrell must spend the next winter in the Mediterranean. As the year advanced the plan matured, and the Archdeacon, knowing how much of Hurrell's heart lay in Newman's keeping, begged him to come and help him with the invalid. Newman spent sleepless nights; where lay his duty? He was free of pupils, but he was Vicar of St. Mary's and its outlying district. England was still in great disorder, and now the cholera was raising its fearful head. If cholera appeared in Oxford Newman could not leave. It did not appear, and the *pros* came to outweigh the *cons*. The Archdeacon engaged berths in the *Hermes*, the largest of the mail-boats, weighing, think of it, eight hundred tons. And they steamed away to the Bay of Biscay on December 7th, 1832.

The travel journals of Froude and Newman reveal some points of interest about the two writers, but mostly careful information which we possess in our Baedekers. They saw nothing of the inner lives of the people they travelled among, and took a deep dislike to the Church of Rome.

They had hit on one of the worst of Mediterranean winters. The winter's rainfall in Sicily, which averages seven inches, was that year thirty-four, and the tour did no good to Hurrell. "Nothing is more common here," writes poor Hurrell, "than sudden change of temperature, and these are the chief occasions of catching cold."

The Archdeacon and Hurrell came home in the spring of 1833, Hurrell delighted to be home again and full of plans of helping the Church. Newman was left behind to make the tour of Sicily on which he had set his heart. There, starvation from bad food, sleeplessness from fleas and other nocturnal enemies, together with very rough travelling, predisposed Newman to the infection of a fever which had become epidemic owing to bad weather.

Newman's account of his illness is one of the most terrible stories of the misfortunes which can befall an inexperienced traveller ever written. We all remember the conviction which remained with him. "I shall not die. I have a work to do in England," and we know that on his way home on board an orange boat bound for Marseilles and becalmed in the Straits of Bonifacio, he wrote "Lead, kindly light."

Owing to the difficulties of international posts in those days it was difficult to get tidings of

Newman, and his friends remained anxious about him until he landed in England on July 10th, 1833. Four days later Keble preached the Assize sermon.

Meanwhile, Hurrell was at home, full of the prospect of doing something for the Church. He was little better, and perhaps felt that his time was short. And so came the day that spring when Hurrell Froude and Isaac Williams walked in the gardens of Trinity, pacing the lime walk where the Court walked when King Charles I was in Oxford, and which the wits had called Daphne.

" Isaac," said Hurrell, " we must make a row in the world, why should we not ? Only consider what the Peculiars " (the Evangelicals of that time) " have done with only a few half truths to work on. And with our principles, if we set resolutely to work, we can do the same."

" I have no doubt," said Isaac, " that we can make a noise and may get people to join us. But shall we make them really better Christians ? If they take up our principles in a hollow way, as the Peculiars have done, then what good shall we do ? "

" Church principles," said Hurrell, decidedly, " must do good. However, we must try. And Newman and I are determined to set to work as soon as he returns, and you must join us. We must have short tracts and letters in the *British Magazine*, and verses, and these you can do for us, and get people to preach on the Apostolic Succession and the like. Let us come and see old Palmer and get him to join us."

So they turn out into the Broad and go through St. Giles and Beaumont Street to Worcester, and find Mr. William Palmer sitting among his battalions of ancient books, who receives them sympathetically but in the reserved, non-committal way in which Dr. Brightman would have received them at Magdalen. " Palmer could not understand Froude," said Isaac Williams, " but he was hearty in our cause."

From this time, says Williams, Hurrell drooped and failed more and more in health of body, and we lost him practically out of Oxford. But his spirit never failed, nor his will. On the 14th of July Keble preached the Assize sermon, but in that sermon the world heard the trumpet tones of Hurrell Froude. Withdrawn bodily from Oxford, his health wavering but never improving, Hurrell Froude had one more task to perform, the task of helping Newman to launch the Tracts for the Times. The great danger now came from the admirable men who agreed with Newman and Froude that something must be done to save the Church, but hoped it might be something which, without upsetting anybody or anything, would guide her feet into the way of peace. They forgot, they always forget, that the Founder of the Church did not find that possible, and that the disciples are not above their Master.

There had to be a bomb. It was Froude's part to help Newman prepare it and fire it. A fortnight after the Assize sermon he met Mr. Hugh James Rose, of Cambridge, the influential editor of the *British Magazine*, Mr. William Palmer and Mr. A. P. Perceval, at Hadleigh Rectory in Suffolk, when he soon saw that if there were to be extreme measures, Newman, Keble and he must discard some of the most respectable of their friends. Their friends wanted a committee ; they knew that there must be a Francis, Savonarola, Luther, Loyola, Wesley, whom you will, but Men, Personalities.

Tracts meant individuals speaking their minds, a committee meant a group finding a formula. Newman and Froude broke away at once with the Tracts. So they were launched. " Very different," says Dean Church, " from anything of the kind yet known in England. They were clear, brief, stern, sparing of words, appeals to conscience and reason, utterly without rhetoric, intense in purpose. They were like the short sharp utterances of men in pain and danger and pressing emergency."

166

Froude wrote three and continued to work from Dartington until the November of 1834. From then until the spring of 1835 he was in the West Indies, mostly in Barbadoes, always with some flickering hope of recovery. He came back to die in 1835, and lingered at home for a year more.

While he lived he appeared always as one who spurs on and incites, while others hesitate. " What fun it is to be living in such times as these," he used to say. " Above the rest of us," his comrades said, " he has the certainty of victory."

And now it is Sunday morning, February 28th, 1836. His father has said the morning office with Hurrell and read a sermon with him. He has noticed how Hurrell has been making it into a meditation. At noon his father brings him some nourishment, but as he bends over his boy he sees that the time for earthly nourishment is passed, there are a few unconscious movements, a few fluttering sighs, and Hurrell is at rest.

Living a short time, he had fulfilled a long time, and having received a good report through faith, received not the promise, God having provided some better thing for us that he without us should not be made perfect.

THE MARTYRDOM OF BISHOP
JOHN COLERIDGE PATTESON

WE have been journeying down the centuries, and this story begins less than a hundred years ago. Queen Victoria has married Prince Albert and has become accustomed to the manners of Sir Robert Peel. These are the hungry 'forties; farm labourers earn twelve shillings a week, bread is two shillings a loaf, tea is eight shillings a pound. But in the scene before us all is gaiety, for it is a lovely July day, and we are watching the opening of the Eton and Harrow match at Lords. Eton has won the toss and has sent in Coley Patteson; he is very popular and has a good reception as he comes on to the ground with the careful nonchalance we know so well. A tall, strong boy, with a dark complexion, very blue eyes, and a charming smile. When he returns to the pavilion at the end of the innings he gets a great ovation, for he is carrying out his bat for fifty, having completely broken the neck of the bowling by steady play.

And now it is the end of the second day, Eton is winning and the last Harrow man has gone in.

He sends Coley in the field a terribly difficult catch, and Coley holds the ball. He has won the match for Eton, and the thunder of human ecstasy rends the sky.

Look at Coley, raised to the highest pinnacle of human glory! He is destined to see greater things than these, and his destiny is already fixed.

It was on the Eve of All Saints, three years before, that Eton parish church saw the most remarkable scene in its history. The curate of Eton was to preach his farewell sermon at the three o'clock evensong, and the parish church was packed from end to end with Eton boys. Somewhere in the pack stands fourteen-year-old Coley Patteson. The curate of the parish church was the idol of Eton; he was a renowned cricketer, he had rowed for Cambridge against Oxford in the first Varsity boat-race; he had got the ban lifted from rowing at Eton and added another thrill to school sport. His tremendous walks were famous; he used to run across ploughed fields to strengthen his wind. He was the most daring cross-country rider in England, no horse could throw him. He would pick out a church spire for his goal and ride at full gallop in a straight line towards it, jumping every obstacle that came in his way.

How could Eton help regarding George Augus-

tus Selwyn with idolatrous feelings! To-morrow
the idol of the school was going away; he was
giving up the highest prospects here to go alone
to the farthest ends of the earth, and transform
ferocious savages into the followers of our Lord.

"The abundance of the sea shall be counted
unto thee" was his text, and Coley listened with
burning cheeks and staring eyes.

Some days afterwards Selwyn went down to
Feniton, the Pattesons' place, near Ottery St. Mary,
to say good-bye to Sir John and Lady Patteson.
They sat round him in the drawing-room after
dinner as he unfolded his plans.

Suddenly Selwyn said, "Lady Patteson, will you
give me Coley?"

There was a silence, and a sword entered that
mother's soul also that the thoughts of many hearts
might be revealed. But God never claimed the
sacrifice. He took her to Himself while the
children were still young, and their father became
father and mother to them. . . .

John Coleridge Patteson, like John the Baptist,
was the gift to our Lord of a beautiful religious
woman. As a child he had a violent temper.
He conquered it through the power of the religion
his mother taught him, and it was in his struggles
with his temper that he got his vocation to the
priesthood. Someone asked him when he was a

small boy : " Coley, why do you want to be a clergyman ? " And he said, " Because I want to make people happy by saying the absolution for them."

Coley had brilliant abilities, though he never quite exercised them to the full at Eton owing to his love of games. He left Eton a sound scholar and captain of the eleven. His last match against Harrow was memorable. Eton went in and got 261. Harrow made 82, followed on and got 55, so Eton won by an innings and 124 runs. But when the Eton captain went up to Balliol and was asked to play for Oxford, he said, " No, I must work." He worked and won a fellowship at Merton, and came to live in the lovely Fellows' Quad, was ordained, and became curate of a hamlet of his home parish, Ottery St. Mary, near Feniton, his father's house. He was intensely happy there. Then one day Selwyn came again. Thirteen years had passed since the Sunday in Eton parish church. Meanwhile Selwyn had created the church of New Zealand and had come home to get its constitution authorized, and to get a new ship for the work in the Melanesian Islands.

Once more Selwyn spoke. " Judge," said the Bishop to Sir John, " will you give me Coley ? "

And the judge said, " I cannot let him go, but God forbid that I should stop him." And as he prayed, the vision of the Pacific won for Christ broke upon him, and he said, "Yes, and mind I give him wholly, not with any thought of seeing him again. I will not have him thinking that he must come back again to see me."

Coley knew his father was right in this. His love for his father and his home was his great passion; he knew he could never bear the strain of coming back for a time, that if he went at all he must go for ever.

At the beginning of 1855 there was a great frost. The Pattesons were all ardent skaters and Coley led the revels on the ice—the last ice he was ever to see—and then on the morning of Lady Day he kissed them all in the doorway of Feniton and went out alone towards the church-yard. He gathered some primroses from his mother's grave and then he went away for ever.

Let us look at the world he was going to. North-east of New Zealand stretches the vast Pacific and the great sprinkling of islands we call Polynesia. Directly north of New Zealand, separated from Polynesia by empty sea, a long splutter of islands stretches up, a thousand miles from the coast of Australia. They are called Melanesia, from the Greek word which means black, because their people are darker than the Polynesians.

Now when Selwyn came to read the legal document which defined his jurisdiction as Bishop of New Zealand, he found that the clerk who engrossed it had made a clerical error. The clerk had written N. 34 instead of S. 34, and Selwyn took the error to be a sign from heaven, for it made him Bishop of the Melanesian Islands. He accepted the call and determined to bring the Gospel to every island where it had never been brought before; yet the problem of how to do it seemed insoluble. These people were so cut off from the rest of the world that they were, practically speaking, on another planet. People who came to them across the vastness of the ocean were to them what visitors from Mars would be to us. Such visitors had come—whalers, sandal-wood traders, hunters for tortoise shell. The whites had vilely misused the islanders, who had come to believe that this monstrous race of whites was a race of devils. And the islands themselves were so scattered that they had little intercourse with one another. Their languages were innumerable: to plant a white man in every island with a knowledge of its language was impossible. What was to be done? Selwyn at his Altar in New Zealand sought the answer and, if we may speak like the Bible, " The Lord said, gather to a home in New Zealand some of the brightest boys from

every group of islands ; keep them for the summer
months of every year, and send them back every
winter to their warmer islands to be missionaries
to their people."

Now that is what Selwyn and his successor,
Patteson, did. I will give you a lightning sketch
of the plan, and, for the rest, tell you some of
the stories of how they did it. They went sailing
through the islands asking boys to come back to
New Zealand and be trained; they founded a
college for them in New Zealand, and through
their love—it was all done by love—brought them
gradually into union with our Lord in His Church
through the sacraments. Every winter the boys
went home across a thousand miles of sea to tell
their people all about the love. " There is a greater
Spirit," they said, " than our Spirits, and He is not
cruel to us as our Spirits are. He loves us and
He has sent His son, Bisope (the Bishop), to love
us and teach us to love one another."

After some years Selwyn divided his jurisdiction
and gave Melanesia to Patteson and they moved
the college to Norfolk Island, six hundred miles
nearer the groups—lovely Norfolk Island, to which
the Pitcairn islanders had been transplanted.
Patteson made this his headquarters. There he
founded his college of St. Barnabas, and there,
surrounded by his Melanesian boys, he spent his

happiest days. From there he went to martyrdom.

Let us try to see it all as Patteson saw it when his Elijah, Selwyn, took the young Elisha for his first voyage in the mission ship. After days of sunshine and a sea of lapis-lazuli, an island rose on the horizon, a hilly island rising like an emerald out of the still waters of a lagoon, surrounded by an outer reef which protected it from the furious battering of the breakers on the shore.

Patteson is fascinated by the palms rising out of the green tangle of undergrowth, the brilliant coral reef, the bright blue fish, the dazzling sparkle of the spray. On the shore are hundreds of natives, heavily armed, showing their excitement at the approach of white men with wild, uncouth cries and gestures. Each native is armed with tetanus, for a mere scratch from one of his poisoned arrows will give it, and in those days there was no antitoxin. They have always regarded white men as devils ; now two are landing. Will the natives kill them before they find that they are angels ? In every case the courage and love of Selwyn and Patteson win the day. Selwyn handles the crowd as a charmer handles a cobra ; one suggestion of fear in Selwyn and his life is forfeit, but he is superman ; the savages click with their tongues their approval of the two of them. These are gods, they say, not men, and they mean well by us.   Both Selwyn and Patteson quickly learned enough of their languages to talk simply to the natives. The diocese of Melanesia is an illustration of that apostolic gift of being understood everywhere which so amazed the world in Apostolic days.

Always the Bishop asked for boys that he might take them away and teach them what would benefit their race, and, amazing to say, he recruited them time after time.   But there were shocks for his Elisha.   A distinguished chief called Iri asks the visitors to his house.   Arrived there he points with pride to twenty-nine nice fresh human skulls, and says, " I got them during my last head-hunting expedition."

" My dear chief," says the Bishop, " I am here to tell you that such acts are wrong.   I am the messenger of the God of Peace."

" My dear Bisope," replies the chief, " I cannot understand how it is that a man of your splendid bodily powers does not appreciate the glory of war.   Nevertheless, I will gladly allow two of my people to return with you to New Zealand to learn what you have to teach them."

Patteson tells us that he would find a village a picture of happy festival.   From all the country-side the people are bringing all sorts of contributions to the feast, the cooking of which is being undertaken by the ladies of the community, and then his eye would fall on the *pièce de résistance*, the body of a plump young man which is being prepared for roasting.

Do not shudder! Cannibals are only unsophisticated pagans. Sacrifice is the law of human life, and cannibalism is only a wrong development of the doctrine of sacrifice carried to its logical conclusion; it is the spiritual exaltation of a cannibal feast which makes it so enchanting. So notwithstanding all this the boys came.

Once Selwyn landed on the island of Nengone tired and thirsty, and asked for water. Siapo, a beautiful young chieftain, a bronze statue, jumped down into a deep cleft to fetch it. The Bishop followed, and bending over the edge saw the laughing, upturned face of the lad, offering him the water bowl. It was Jacob's Well, and the Bishop, meeting the boy's eyes, prayed passionately that our Lord would give Siapo the living water.

After a little time Siapo came to him and said, " I am coming with you to learn, and I am bringing four of my friends." The Bishop said he found him a princely lad with the makings of a great missionary. Then God called him to Himself and it is in the Beatific Vision that Siapo works to-day.

Once when Patteson was approaching the island of Melanta a great war canoe approached the mission ship. Thirty-six glorious youths were at

the oars sending the beautiful boat skimming like
a bird over the water. Utterly fascinated, Patteson
watched their rhythm, while he remembered what
they were going to do : before dawn next day,
with blood-curdling yells, they would fall on
some sleeping village and rush upon it in a whirl-
wind of massacre. Then he sprang into his dinghy
and rowed out into their path. They paused on
their oars and bent keen, fierce eyes on him. In
broken words he preached to them the love of
our Father Who is in heaven. Two faces softened ;
without a word two of the most attractive lads
jumped out of the war canoe and came to him
over the water. Just think of the joy in Coley's
heart as he carried them away.

During one of his first voyages Selwyn had
seen a tiny canoe blown out to sea towards his
vessel, and found it contained a little boy on the
point of collapsing in a hopeless battle with wind
and sea. Selwyn saved him, fed him and put him
to bed. The small boy soon fell asleep, but would
now and then wake up and search for his paddle
that he might go on fighting the waves, and then
with a huge sigh of relief cuddle down again.
Next morning Selwyn sent him back to his village
with presents and words of goodwill. Years
afterwards Patteson landed on that shore to find
himself clasped in the arms of Selwyn's waif, now

a strong lithe lad. He would not leave Patteson, and even when they were back on the mission boat Taroniara clung to him still.

Again a long time passed, and one day in the mission college Taroniara went into the Bishop's room and said, "Bishop, why is it that I now think what I never thought before? I know I may be wrong, but I don't think I shall ever listen to people trying to take me from you and the teaching. I like, and wish for things I never used to want, and I don't care now for things I used to want and live for; what is it?"

"What do you think it is?" said the Bishop.

"I think, but this is so *mava*, so great, I think it is the Spirit of God in my heart."

It was for this that Patteson gave up all else, and at length there came a day when he completed his sacrifice.

As the work of the white angels grew, so did the work of the white devils. The enslaving, outraging and murdering of the islanders by the white scum of the Pacific increased, and blood for blood still remained the law of those islanders who did not know our Lord.

It was the twentieth of September, 1870, and the *Southern Cross*, with the Bishop on board, was approaching the island of Nukapu. He was teaching the Acts to his boys and closed the book with the martyrdom of St. Stephen. There had been fresh outrages by the whites in the islands, and the Bishop knew there was a risk in landing, but he landed. He landed alone and disappeared into the screen of foliage at the back of the beach. Then natives on the shore shot at the boats and wounded the Bishop's companions. No one could land to help the Bishop for some time, as the tide was too low to cross the reef. When the tide had risen, at half-past-four, two canoes were launched from the shore on the calm lagoon, and after a while one loosed the other and put back, while the loosed canoe floated on towards the Bishop's companions in the ship's boats. They thought it was a trap, and expected a figure to rise from the boat and shoot. But there was no movement in the boat. Then, very gently, they lifted the wrappings which concealed the boat's contents. On the floor of the canoe lay the body of the Bishop, laid out with all reverence. A smile of perfect peacefulness illuminated his face. He was wrapped in white matting of exquisite texture; his hands were crossed upon his breast, and in them he held a palm branch, every leaf of which was knotted. It was the symbol of the Avenger of Blood. Five natives had been killed, and on the body of the Bishop the Avenger had imprinted Five Wounds.

A HUNDRED YEARS IN
MARGARET STREET

IN the eighteenth century Bloomsbury must have looked like Bath, fine houses and green fields adjacent. After a time came Cavendish Square, with feelers running out into the country, and a big gap between it and Bloomsbury. There was a farm where Berners Street is now, and the town stopped with the good houses in Margaret Street. These ended with Great Titchfield Street and beside the little lane in the angle of which is the All Saints' Parish Hall—Marylebone Passage—there was nothing between Great Titchfield Street and the farm. The gap was filled by streets of a lower class, the sort of streets with which big houses become fringed—livery stables, dog fanciers, small shops, mews, and generally the sort of slums which places like Cavendish Square breed.

Margaret Street was prolonged in two lines of middle-class houses in cheap imitation of the better sort, and became a street of lodging houses frequented by the lesser gentry when they came to town. For example, Mr. Jarndyce of *Bleak House* evidently stayed at 21, and it was from the entrance to Marylebone Passage that Mr. Guppy gazed in adoration at Miss Esther Summerson. Later on, when the church was built, the lodging houses used to take in what we call our country congregation. Those opposite the church were strung together and made the Mother House of the All Saints' Community, and others came into the hands of the Sisters and were used for their various works of mercy.

For a hundred years or so before the foundation of the church was laid there stood a hideous little building surrounded first by slums and then by lodgings—Margaret Chapel.

Margaret was the only child of John Holles, Duke of Newcastle. She married William Bentinck, Duke of Portland, and from the names of the Mortimers, Portlands, Oxfords and Bentincks came Portland Place, Oxford Street, Cavendish Square, Holles Street, Bentinck Street, Duke Street, Duchess Street, and Margaret Street. This will be news for the cheeky boys at Kelham, who, I am told, call us St. Margaret's, Mowbray Street, for our amiable young lady of quality was never a saint.

In the latter part of the eighteenth century, David Williams, founder of the Literary Fund, came to London. He had been a Dissenting Minister at Frome, in Exeter, and at Highgate. In 1776 he cut himself off from Christianity and opened a small

mean chapel in Margaret Street, Cavendish Square,
"for public worship on the Principles of Natural
Religion apart from Revelation." He produced a
prayer book from which the name of Christ was
expunged, and published two quarto volumes
entitled *Lectures on the Universal Principles and
Duties of Religion and Morality as they have been read
in Margaret Street, Cavendish Square, in the years* 1776
and 1777 *by the Reverend David Williams* (*with portrait
of the Author*). But Mr. Williams did not succeed,
the congregation dwindled, and Margaret Chapel
was closed. It is said to have been run for a short
time by people called "Bereans," but this was a
flash in the pan. Margaret Chapel was re-opened
as a proprietary chapel of the Church of England,
and for some twenty years the Reverend J. D.
Hazelwood was its minister. It evidently had a
good backing of prosperous people like old Miss
Crawley if she ever went to Church, Sir Pitt, and
Arthur Pendennis, and Colonel Newcombe. Like
Charles Honeyman's chapel in *The Newcomes* it
actually had wine vaults in the crypt, which
remained there until Frederick Oakeley cleared
them out.

Towards the end of the 'Twenties the little
building embarked upon a venture which was
destined to come to nothing. Henry Drummond,
the banker, was a leader in the Irvingite Movement

which began in the Presbyterian Body, and which
felt itself to be a movement blest and inspired by
the Holy Ghost and designed to restore the fire
and force of primitive Christianity in modern times.
Henry Drummond bought the lease and site of
Margaret Chapel to establish it as a centre from
which to propagate Irvingism inside the communion of the Church of England. He appointed
Mr. William Dodsworth, an Anglican Priest who
was licensed as Minister on March 6th, 1829. The
idea was not to drift from Anglicanism, but to
leaven it with Catholic Apostolic ideas, just as
to-day it would be possible to use a London Church
for developing Group Movement ideas in an
Anglican parish. But we have no evidence that
this ever happened. The poor little Chapel was
soon seen to be unfit for any big development, and
Mr. Dodsworth's friends set about building Christ
Church, Albany Street, for his occupation. Meanwhile a more earnest and vigorous churchmanship
was developed in Margaret Street. We hear of
Sunday and Saints' Day Eucharists. It attracted
such important clergymen as Mr. Samuel Wilberforce, and the work demanding an assistant minister,
Mr. Upton Richards, of Exeter College, Oxford,
was appointed. Mr. Richards remained in this
subordinate post when Mr. Dodsworth went to
Christ Church, Albany Street, in 1837. He

remained on through the short time when the
delicate and learned Mr. Thornton was incumbent
and through the whole of Mr. Oakeley's time, and
helped him to make Margaret Chapel the centre of
Tractarian life and worship in London.

At the great crisis in 1845, when Oakeley seceded
to Rome with Newman, the devoted members of
the congregation, who were determined to save
the work in Margaret Street, prevailed on the
Bishop of London to appoint Upton Richards to
the Incumbency, and so that gentle fair-haired,
smiling man, with the rare gift of drawing sympathizers to help him in his undertakings, and the
still rarer gift of interior quiet, of not being upset
by upsetting things, became the Founder of All
Saints', Margaret Street.

Whether Mr. Williams adapted a building and
turned it into Margaret Chapel, or whether he
actually built the poor little place to be the temple
of natural religion, I have not been able to discover.
It stood where the courtyard is now, an oblong
room flush with the street, with two doors opening
on to the pavement, facing, therefore, North and
South, and not East and West. The pulpit must
have faced the street from about the middle block
of the men's seats in the present nave. It was
hideous (I am quoting Oakeley), an oblong room,
low, dark and stuffy, with a whitewashed flat roof

and two large galleries filled on Sundays with uneasy school children, and the whole area covered with pews ; no central passage, only two side ones ; the end wall flat and plain. In the middle of the chapel towards the further end rose the three decker ; the clerk's desk, the reading desk, the pulpit piled one above the other. Behind the three decker, against the end wall, a small mean table did duty for Altar. The pews were made of deal and showed traces of having been painted in days gone by. By the most ingenious cramming the place could not hold more than two hundred and fifty persons.

To this place, on the 5th July, 1839, came the Reverend Frederick Oakeley, Senior Fellow of Balliol, and Prebendary of Lichfield. Kind, good, lovable, scholar-like and gentle, *distrait*, quiet, silent, a thin short limping figure with dark hair closely cropped, good features, bright eyes and square shaped head. "Frederick Oakeley was an elegant writer and a great lover of music," writes Benjamin Jowett years after, " and much respected by us."

For ten years Oakeley had lived in Oxford in the thick of the Movement, and he came to London with the object of expressing its principles in the ritual and devotional life of an Anglican Church and congregation. It had become known that he wished to do this, and he was offered Margaret Chapel. A more unpromising sphere for carrying out such a project could not be imagined, and Oakeley afterwards said that looking back he found it hard to master the state of mind under which he accepted the offer. But Dodsworth had left the nucleus of a promising congregation under Upton Richards, and Oakeley set to work. He began by getting rid of the three decker and making a small pulpit on one side and a small reading desk on the other. It was more difficult to get rid of the parish clerk, for the office was a freehold and the clerk behaved like a bishop deprived of his throne. He tried to re-establish his desk first in one part of the chapel and then in another, and continued to yell out the responses in the old style and in the loudest and most discordant fashion.

Oakeley placed the poor little Altar against the end wall and placed the Bible, bound in two volumes of red morocco, leaning against the wall at the Gospel and Epistle ends. He inserted a little coloured glass in the end windows, and enclosed the Altar in a semicircular rail.

Such was All Saints' in its first state. Here Mr. Oakeley established an admirable congregational service, and collected round him a most zealous and devout body of people. The first thing he attempted was the collection of the alms every

Sunday, and then offering them at the Altar in the Prayer for the Church Militant. This was the only change contemplated at first in the service; coloured frontals varying with the seasons were gradually introduced, and pulpit hangings of unusual richness for festivals. Natural flowers were woven into wreaths and garlands for festivals, or placed upon the Altar, and an attempt was made that their colours, white or red, should harmonize with the season. Two candles were put upon the Altar; later they were bright green, but it was feared to give offence by lighting them. Still less possible was it to wear the proper vestments. Persons were taught to bow towards the Altar in passing it. It was thought consistent with the rubric to consecrate at the centre of the Altar, although other portions of the service would be recited at the north and south ends. The alms and oblations it was felt should be offered in a kneeling posture.

Between 1837 and 1845, when Mr. Oakeley followed Mr. Newman to Rome, things remained very much like this, but behind Mr. Oakeley stood Mr. William George Ward, all the time Oakeley's greatest friend and a most powerful, masterful character. Ward often stayed with Oakeley, who had an oratory in his house at 74 Margaret Street, and here many offices were said in addition to the

Prayer Book ones. Oakeley, who was a musical genius, had made the music in the chapel very good. He was the first man to produce a Gregorian edition of the Canticles and Psalter, which were chanted in alternate verses by the officiant and a choirboy in a surplice who stood by his side, and the choir in the front row of the gallery. I gather that during these years, in addition to the congregations which filled the Chapel on Sundays and Saints' Day, there was a growing inner circle in which W. G. Ward made himself much felt, and who supplemented the Prayer Book services with other offices in the Oratory. This was a section of the very definitely Romanizing section of the Movement, and it carried Oakeley with it, leaving behind Upton Richards and the bulk of the Sunday and Saints' Days congregations. The younger Clergy used to bring their young people from all sides to Evensong on weekdays, and many merchants would come to Mattins before they went to business, and get away in time for Evensong, and of course there were many leisured people, male and female, who found Margaret Chapel a new interest. A few years ago Mr. Richard Gledhill, who had been a choirboy in the Chapel in those days, and who died in his hundredth year, spent part of a Festival with us. At the large luncheon Mr. Henry William Brooke gave to the old choristers at the Berners Hotel,

Mr. Gledhill made a speech and revived the feeling caused by Oakeley's secession. It was a most interesting experience; we were made to feel by one of the people the agony it caused and the anti- or perhaps rather non-Roman feeling it left behind. Oakeley became a Roman Catholic in October, 1845.

Something had to be done to secure a future for Margaret Chapel. It was a private leasehold property held under the Crown still in the name of Mr. Drummond, the Irvingite, and the lease had only two years to run, when the property would revert to the Crown. Mr. J. D. Chambers, the Recorder of Salisbury, made himself responsible for the ground rent, and the congregation bound themselves into an association to keep the Chapel open. The leaders were Mr. Henry Tritton and Mr. Beresford Hope. They approached Bishop Blomfield, who agreed to license Mr. Upton Richards as Minister of the Chapel, with the under-standing that he would continue the service on the existing lines. The Chapel was dilapidated and almost ruinous, and the first thing to do was to restore it and improve its fittings. The work was finished by All Saints-tide, 1846, when the Chapel presented the appearance it does in the little drawing in the Vicarage, which represents the last Epiphany Eucharist in it before it was pulled down in the beginning of 1850.

It is constantly being forgotten that the artistic and ritual aspect of the Oxford Movement began in Cambridge and was started by the Cambridge Camden Society, which expanded into the Ecclesiological Society, whose chief object at the beginning was to build a model church in London to exhibit to the world the most perfect example of the worship of the Church of England in a building which should embody the highest ideas attainable of Christian art. Mr. Beresford Hope was the moving spirit in this, and when in 1845 a future had to be found for Margaret Chapel it seemed natural to think of it as the providential opportunity for building the model church.

It was felt to be a thrilling idea. Upton Richards issued a stimulating appeal, the Bishop consented, Sir Stephen Glynne and Beresford Hope undertook to act as sub-committee and procure plans, and the circular went out on February 10th, 1847, to persons known to be interested in the idea. The site of Margaret Chapel and the adjoining three houses was bought for £9,000. Mr. Butterfield was selected as architect, and steps were taken to constitute an ecclesiastical parish under the title of All Saints'.

From 1849 to 1850 the services were continued in the old Chapel. Mr. Hope took upon himself the burden of the temporary arrangements. He took two houses in Titchfield Street, fitted up the big room, which one of them contained, to be the temporary Chapel, and collected the Assistant Clergy and Choristers into the rest of the buildings. Mr. Hope paid the rent and taxes and helped largely with all the running expenses. On Low Sunday evening, April 7th, 1850, the last sermon was preached in Margaret Chapel by the Reverend Charles Marriott, Fellow of Oriel. He said, " We cannot but love these poor walls and leave them with some of the regret with which we part for a while from the earthly tenement of an immortal spirit. Still we must rejoice that after our poor manner of imitating the works of Him Who created us in His own image, we hope to be able to restore them with a renewed identity and something of the form and beauty which befits their heavenly use."

On Monday, April 8th, Mass was celebrated for the last time. It is a solemn *memento mori* for All Saints', Margaret Street, that the choir of St. Andrew's, Wells Street, volunteered *en masse* and joined with the choir of the Chapel in singing Mattins at seven, followed by the Liturgy. One who was present says that the emotion of the congregation could never be forgotten, that the *Amen* to the last Pax and Blessing vibrated through the building, that the majority were in tears, and many pressed their lips to the woodwork of the poor

little building. When I see the shop girls and
office boys, the strangers and passers-by entering
All Saints' all day long, and bowing down in prayer,
I realize that that Pax and Blessing of old Margaret
Chapel have gone on vibrating down all the years.

All Saints' is built on a square; a hundred feet
each way, shut in on three sides. Ruskin says of
it, " It is the first piece of architecture I have seen
built in modern days which is free from all signs of
timidity or incapacity. In general proportion of
parts, in refinement—piquancy of mouldings,
above all in force—and grace of floral ornament,
worked in a broad and vigorous manner, it chal-
lenges fearless comparison with the noblest work
of any time." George Edmund Street, the great
architect, who for years was one of our Church-
wardens, says of the church, " Though I have a
rather large acquaintance with English and foreign
works executed since the revival of pointed art, I
cannot hesitate for a moment in allowing that this
church is not only the most beautiful but the most
vigorous, thoughtful and original of them all."
And Mr. Comper, who has done the most important
work in our church during the last twenty years,
said to me when he began to restore the East
wall and erect the Lady Altar, " When I look at
Butterfield's proportions I sometimes feel there is
no one else." We must not let the fussy decora-

tion which we regret blind us to the grandeur of the whole design.

Dr. Pusey laid the foundation stone on All Saints' Day, 1850. It was the year when the Pope parcelled out England into Roman Catholic dioceses, and the anti-papal rage of the populace was tempted to vent itself on everything Catholic it could find. If it had been generally known that Dr. Pusey was coming to lay the stone, it was feared that a Protestant mob would have wrecked Margaret Street. So the stone was laid with as little noise as possible and the work began.

The shell was built in two years. Then the funds available at the moment were exhausted, and the work was stopped for two years. Meanwhile the temporary Chapel got crowded out, and in 1854 two parallel efforts were started. Mr. Upton Richards set to work to collect funds to build a larger temporary chapel, and Mr. Beresford Hope made a separate effort to complete All Saints' Church.

Next year Mr. Richards opened what was afterwards known as the Confraternity Chapel at 77 Margaret Street, opposite the church gates. It was a good, dignified building, very much better than what had gone before. When the church was consecrated the Sisters retained the Chapel for the use of the Confraternities. I often said Mass in

it when I was first ordained, and on my first Good
Friday I performed the Stations of the Cross in it,
followed by a procession of dying penitents, the
patients who were fatally diseased ; a very poignant
memory. Here in the five years before the church
was consecrated a big work of teaching, preaching
and shriving was carried on. This big spiritual
work was carried bodily into the new church on
May 28th, 1859.

It was very difficult to keep a steadfast staff at
work, and the clergy were constantly changing.
But in 1857 Mr. Charles Henry Christie joined the
staff and remained until 1886. Christie was one of
the saints of the Catholic Revival, and he was a
pillar of this work. Men of similar calibre were
Charles Gutch, who came here when the church
was consecrated and was the founder of St.
Cyprian's, Clarence Gate, and Richard Temple
West, who came the year after, and who founded
St. Mary Magdalene's, Paddington. Arthur Brinckman was lightly attached to All Saints' for many
years while he did his great penitentiary work. I
knew Christie, West, who offered me a curacy, and
Brinckman, who has preached here since I have
been Vicar. A woman who had known him here
forty years before, and had been in Australia ever
since, came back that night to see the old church.
Not knowing that a service was going on she pushed

open the door, and lo and behold her old friend, Arthur Brinckman, was standing in the pulpit.

Funds failed the first Choir School in 1852, and it was dissolved; another Choir of local boys was attempted in 1856, but it only lasted two years. Redhead had been the first organist. Our present Choir was collected for the Consecration in 1859, and fully constituted in 1860. This year Mr. Willing became the organist. He was Oakeley's boy in the surplice, and to him we owe the beautiful responses in Advent and Lent. The first choirboy, Henry William Brooke, died two or three years ago. He was head of Novello's, and our loyal and generous friend. He gave the old boys a great luncheon at the Festival year after year, and kept many old fellows in touch with us, among them H. W. Rowdon, Priest Vicar for many years of Lichfield Cathedral, who came here, I think, in 1862, and remained our devoted friend to the end of his life which closed the other day. I like to remember that he sat with us in Choir at the last Festival of his life on earth.

Well, the church was consecrated on May 28th, 1859, by Tait, Bishop of London. He had passed everything except the Altar Cross, which was a highly-coloured affair attached to the East wall. The Bishop objected that it looked as if it were standing on the Altar and had the lower limb hacked off. He had also never seen an Altar with a fair linen which did not envelope it; before beginning the Service he sent for Mr. Richards and demanded a table-cloth, so two were produced from 74 Margaret Street, and the poor Altar was entirely concealed from view. Otherwise all went well.

The Ecclesiastical Commissioners had refused at first to accept the church because of the expense of the two houses, 7 and 8 Margaret Street, but it was pointed out that this is one house with a common basement containing its offices. Since I have been Vicar the authorities have overthrown this and insisted on rating us as two—a matter I should like our borough councillor to enquire into.

Mr. Beresford Hope gave the site, Mr. Tritton built the church and its surroundings—it cost £60,000; Lord Sligo gave the Baptistry; and Mr. Benjamin Lancaster gave the endowment, which was designedly as small as possible in order that the Incumbent might remain entirely in the hands of the congregation, who could starve him out at any moment. On the 28th of May, £3,000 was still wanted for the fittings, but the enthusiasm of the moment may be gathered from the fact that £2,800 was given during the octave. The collection at the High Mass on the Day of the Consecration was £2,196 18s. 2d.

Prebendary Whitworth quotes the effect it had on a poor business boy who came from Finsbury the Sunday after. When he awoke next morning he thought at first he had dreamt it, he had never seen anything so unearthly, so devout. He became a devoted Churchman and made his first Confession here, often walking eighteen miles to the Sunday morning service. Then he went to the Colonies, offered himself to be ordained, and became a dignitary in the Church abroad. "This," Prebendary Whitworth adds, "was the impression made on the first multitudes."

From 1859 to 1873, when Mr. Richards died, the work rolled steadily on, maintaining its character and keeping on the same lines. Edgar Hoskins was here from 1863 to 1881, and he is said to have compiled the *Treasury of Devotion* in what is now my bedroom. The Eucharistic vestments were introduced at High Mass on Sunday, August 11th, 1867, eight years after the Consecration. That year George Edmund Street, the great architect, became Churchwarden, a post he held for four years. It was he who was mainly instrumental in getting the vestments worn. The Three Hours service was introduced that year too, preceded by the Reproaches.

During those years the congregation were busy building 84 Margaret Street. They had hitherto

carried on the Parochial Schools under great difficulties in Great Titchfield Street. And meanwhile
the All Saints' Community had been growing
strong, taking up the houses opposite the church
and cleverly knitting them into a Mother House.
To start with they were a great department of
All Saints', and such they remained during Mr.
Richards' lifetime. Since 1873 they have had their
own Chaplain, first Father Benson, and afterwards
one of the Cowley Community. In Mr. Berdmore
Compton's day we did not serve their Altar;
we became their sub-Chaplains in Mr. Whitworth's
time. We serve their Altar and they take charge
of ours ; they still control our large young women's
Confraternity. Their chapel is the original one,
a very beautiful, modest one, with a fine fresco
by Dyce on the East wall, welded now into the
buildings of All Saints' Home, which is a branch
house. The Confraternity Chapel was given up
when they moved their Mother House to St. Albans,
and began to move their institutions. It was turned
for a time into a fencing school, and then was pulled
down. Mother Harriet Brownlow Byron, the
foundress, was, like Mother Harriet Monsell,
Mother Marion Hughes, and Mother Lydia Sellon,
a woman of heroic character. The Mother Foundress began by tending a little home in Mortimer
Street for the incurable and the orphan. When it

was determined to form a Sisterhood, Bishop Wilberforce was commissioned to profess her in the Chapel in Margaret Street, and the Community grew apace. They took charge of our parish, then full of poor, and soon had one hundred and forty members of their household. At 74 Margaret Street, once the Vicar's house, they accommodated sixty-six orphans ; at 77 Margaret Street twenty-five girls who bore the queer name of "Industrial girls" ; at St. Elizabeth's three houses in Mortimer Street, they had a hospital for incurables; at 3 Margaret Street, a hospital for women suffering from advanced cases of venereal disease cared for by Father Brinckman ; and at 4 Margaret Street a home for little incurable boys. They spread throughout Great Britain to Edinburgh, Bradford, Wolverhampton, Eastbourne, St. Leonards, Oxford, Liverpool, Beckenham, Lewisham and Leeds, also to the United States, Cape Town, and Bombay. All this work drew people to its source, as the church was much more interesting when it was frequented by the religious and their people. In 1871 the Mother headed a band of Sisters on to the battlefields of Europe, and nursed the sick and wounded in the Franco-German war.

On March 1st, 1868, Mr. Willing retired, and Mr. William Stevenson Hoyte took his place. When he entered upon his work the Choir knew three anthems and two masses. Three years after they were singing twenty-nine masses.

Soon after, Upton Richards' health broke. He was seized with paralysis and died on June 12th, 1873, after receiving the last Sacraments in peace. He was a great Pastor of Souls, a great organizer, and a great Parish Priest. He was not a learned man and not a great preacher, but he was most winning and affectionate; a man greatly beloved. They said he had always loved the Oxford Movement through its personalities. He never changed his relations with Newman and Keble, who often stayed here with him. None of us can imagine the desolation with which his death overwhelmed the congregation, who saw the whole work destroyed.

The Anglo-Romans made one of their most discreditable efforts. " The All Saints' people are coming so fast," they said, " that we are seriously considering if we had better not fix one particular day to receive the congregation *en masse*. All Saints' is quite done for; like all things which are rotten it must have its end." Arthur Brinckman and his fellow clergy were always hearing this sort of thing. He says that at the outside, between June, when Richards died, and All Saints' Day, when Berdmore Compton was inducted, six people went over.

Berdmore Compton, who was a Fellow of my old College of Merton, had been eight years Rector of St. Paul's, Covent Garden. He had taken a First at Oxford and was a cultured, polished and distinguished gentleman of the old school. No one was better calculated to steer this ship safely through dangerous times, and to enable the nervous bishops to sleep o' nights. I often met him and heard him preach, and marked the profound respect with which he was received when he came back to preach here after his retirement in May, 1886.

Almost directly after Mr. Compton's appointment the great London Mission throughout the Diocese was held in Septuagesima, 1874. Mr. Thorold, afterwards Bishop of Winchester, and Mr. Compton were appointed its secretaries. This naturally drew All Saints' into the centre of things, and gave it that episcopal tinge which has ever adhered to it, and for a time distinguished it from St. Alban's, Holborn. During this period the north wall of the nave was decorated as we see it now, in memory of the first Vicar. Later the west wall formed a memorial of Mr. Compton's incumbency; the great arch of the Baptistry was decorated after my first period here in memory of Lady Powell's father, Mr. Henry Wood, so long our Churchwarden. In 1880 they affixed a marble retable to the reredos, and, I imagine, began to erect large flower vases on it, and Mr. Compton began the first great effort after ritual conformity. It was the big effort of the second generation, and it met in the room the acolytes now use, which we call the " Vicar's room," because in the old days, when the Vicar did not reside in the Clergy house, he used it as his office on the spot. The Conference taught people knowledge, but it did not teach them conformity. It met forty-eight times and was strongly Sarum, but did not make the party so.

Nothing impresses me so much in looking into the past of All Saints' as the amount of renovation it has required. The east wall fell early into ruins. In twenty-six years the cleansing had become a serious business. " There is statuary marble in it," we are told, " which is as black as ebony, and cleansing of this extent involves the erection of scaffolding throughout the entire church up to its highest points." This circular brings us down to the names of my own time, Captain Le Marchant, Major Ruddell Todd, Sir Herbert Barnard, Mr. Fraser Churchill, and Mr. George Lawson, Colonel Lawson's father. Next year, Mr. Compton, now advancing in years, resigned.

All Saints' had always felt it its duty to be faithful and strict to its principles on strictly conservative lines. I fancy it wanted a jolt in 1886, and Bishop

Temple was exactly the man to give it one. All Saints' had had two wealthy Vicars who lived with their own families, at some distance from the church. Bishop Temple appointed Mr. Allen Whitworth, the Vicar of St. John's, Hammersmith, a Fellow of his Cambridge College, and a first-class mathematician, who was married and had no private means, and who, like his present successor, had no musical knowledge or ability whatever. At the moment it caused some stir and a little friction, but the result was very healthy. The services remained much the same, but Mr. Whitworth immediately brought All Saints' up to date over the Sacrament of Penance. I remember the Archdeacon of Berkshire telling me that he made his confession here in the Vestry in his youth, and that the clergy were so careful that if one of them had to go to the door and look out he took off his surplice before he did so. Mr. Whitworth swept this all away and put up notices of Confession in the Church. His first assistant Priest, Father Stafforth, became a great and experienced Confessor. The second thing he did was to attach to All Saints' the Mission in White Lion Street, Pentonville, which was subsequently worked for so long by Father Preedy, and is now in the hands of Father Llewelyn Davies. In 1889 he accepted me to work at Pentonville with my licence to All Saints', and I

began my ministry on Christmas Day by flinging
two hulking girls out of the Mission Chapel, after
which we sang "Hark the herald," and they
screamed on the mat. They were afterwards con-
verted by the Stations of the Cross in Lent and
became the jolliest of girls. Much good was done
by the Mission and still remains. It could not be
worked from here continuously, communications
were too difficult.

Soon after the Mission started we began the
Mission here for the Welsh in West London. In
those days All Saints' had an Evensong at four, the
one the Prince and Princess of Wales attended when
in London, and another thinly attended, at seven.
Between, the Welsh had a sung Evensong at five,
with a bun fight afterwards in the Parish Room,
presided over by Sister Catherine, the great-niece
of Isaac Williams, the boy who went with Hurrell
Froude to John Keble at Southrop. Mr. Whitworth made Killin Roberts our Chaplain, a charming Welshman who used to sing the prayers in a
lovely *hwyl*, and afterwards became Vicar of St.
Andrew's, Hertford. It was he and I who broached
the idea of the Welsh Evensong at St. Paul's on St.
David's Day to the Archdeacon of London, when
I was ordained Priest at Fulham. We carried home
the collection to my rooms at 84 and never saw so
much copper in our lives. The Welsh Church was

built soon afterwards in West London, and our service was no longer needed.

In 1890 came the Lincoln Judgment. Mr. Whitworth considered that All Saints' should conform to it, and did. I resigned and went to Randall at All Saints', Clifton—the Bishop of Gloucester and Bristol having forbidden his clergy to conform to the Lincoln Judgment. I fancy that in his Diocese Bishop King conformed to it. On the only occasion on which I had to act as his Chaplain outside his Diocese he did not.

It was in 1905 that Mr. Whitworth passed away, profoundly respected by all who knew him, and leaving four sons of the finest character to follow him, one of whom has been with us very often during my time, and is one of our closest friends— Father Cyril Whitworth of the S.S.J.E.

This brings us down to our own time, for George Frederick Holden, who came from St. John the Evangelist's, Wilton Road, was only here three years. Holden was, I fancy, more like Upton Richards than anyone else who succeeded him. He always said he was, and I think he was. Everybody loved him. It was impossible not to. He at once began the work of schooling the people towards fasting Communion, and telling them that nobody might communicate at midday unless he had sent his name in the day before. This stopped the people querying, "Shall we go up?" I carried on the same plan when I followed him, and gradually after-breakfast Communion died a natural death. Holden also began carrying the Blessed Sacrament to the sick, and it was the first thing I did on the morning of my institution from the Tabernacle in the Sisters' Oratory.

The green candles on the Altar disappeared, and Micklethwayte designed six of a truly hideous pattern, which the dear Vicar conveyed with stealth one night into church long after dark. There was a thurible too in the Vestry which had not appeared in his lifetime. It came into use during my first Advent, and was used cautiously for the Litany of the Four Last Things. The head of the Men's Guild could not face it at first, and used to leave the church and wait outside the door until the Litany was over, and then return to receive the Blessing. We had that particular thurible silvered lately, and used it. The Altar ornaments Sir Thomas Dick Lauder found for us in Florence, and Micklethwayte's six only appear now among the furniture of the Altar of Repose.

When I asked the Bishop to come and preach on our seventy-fourth anniversary, I said to him, " All Saints', Margaret Street, has never had a row with a Bishop of London, but," I added, " I am not sure that that is to its credit."